Contents

Coaching Linebackers:
By the Experts

Edited by
Earl Browning

ISBN: 1-58518-867-0
Library of Congress Control Number: 2003108311
Cover design: Kerry Hartjen
Text design: Jeanne Hamilton
Front cover photo: Mark Lyons/Getty Images

Coaches Choice
P.O. Box 1828
Monterey, CA 93942
www.coacheschoice.com

Linebacker Drills and Techniques

Barry Alvarez
University of Wisconsin
1990

It is certainly a pleasure to be here today. I can tell you it is tough to follow Coach Lou Holtz as a speaker. He is one of the best speakers in the country. I did welcome the opportunity to sit down and talk with him again. I haven't talked with Lou since the Orange Bowl. As I came in the back of the room tonight, I was asked if he was like this every day. I have listened to him for the last three years and I can tell you it has been like that every day. I believe in him and the players believe in him. That is how things work. Some people may think Lou Holtz was hard to work for. I did not find that at all. If you follow the principles that he talked about, you don't have anything to worry about.

I can remember the first time I interviewed with Lou Holtz. He asked me about goal setting. I told him when I thought about setting goals it reminded me of my grandfather. I never had a chance to meet my grandfather, but my father told me about him. He came to this country from Spain in 1917. He landed in New York when he was only 16 years old. He set a goal for himself at that time. He said he wanted to be a millionaire within 12 months. Eleven months later, he achieved his goal. The amazing thing about all of this is that my grandfather only knew three words of English. Those three words were "stick 'em up." Coach Holtz and I always got along.

My topic is linebacker play. I want to talk about things we believe in. I was a high school coach for nine years before going to Iowa, and then to Notre Dame. I am not trying to sell you on anything we do. I do not know if our way is the right way, or even the best way, but it is what we believe in. If you believe in it, and your players believe in it, you have got a chance to be successful.

A year ago, I spoke in Dallas at a clinic. On that same program was Lloyd Carr of Michigan and Dave Wannstedt of Miami. We all three talked about what we believed in. We all three taught things differently. We all taught different techniques, but we were ranked one, two, and three in the country on defense. That made me think a great deal. There are a lot of different ways to get the job done. The first thing you must do is to be sound. You have to have a sound plan. You have to believe in it and you have to know it. Your coaches have to believe in it and they have to know it. After the coaches get on the same page, you can make your players believe in your plan. The players must believe that their plan is as good as, or better than, any team they will play against. However, the first thing I told the kids at Wisconsin is that they would never take the field where they were not prepared as well as the people they were going to play against. I told them, "You will always have a chance." I learned that you do not win with a plan; you win with the execution by the players.

To have a good defense, the first thing you must do is to select your linebackers. When I played at Nebraska, I was told that I was too slow and that I was not tall enough to play linebacker. But I did enough things well that I was voted All-Big Eight. If I can teach our linebackers some of the things I was asked to do, they could be great players, because I know they are better athletes than I was.

If I had to choose one way to pick a linebacker, it would be to have a scrimmage. I would pick the kid who made the most tackles and make him my linebacker. That is probably going to be the player with the most desire to get to the football. When I sit down to watch films of players, I do not watch technique. I do not even want to know the number of the kid that I am supposed to watch. I watch the film and notice the player who always ends up around the football. Then I like to see what happens when he gets to the ball. I want players to get to the ball in a nasty mood. If a linebacker chases the ballcarrier all the way across the field and doesn't end up on the tackle, then he does not have the attitude to play linebacker. I am not talking about being dirty by spearing the ballcarrier. I am talking about being aggressive. If the ballcarrier is going down and the man pulls off and runs away from the pile, I do not think he has the right temperament to play linebacker. Several years ago, the San Diego Chargers did a personality profile on each football position. They found linebackers had the profile of an assassin. A good linebacker is a kid who thinks he should be involved in every play.

This is what I tell our linebackers. I tell them to take care of their responsibility first and then get to the football. A good linebacker feels like this: If the ball is on the move, he should be doing something to stop the play. That is the attitude I want in my linebackers. I think the linebacker should be an extension of the defensive coach. He should be a smart football player. The coach should work with him to make him a smart football player. I never give the linebacker a set alignment. If you do a good job of teaching the linebacker, and he does a good job of listening, he will adjust to the situations on the field. He should be trained in situations. He should know down and distance, *who* he is playing against, and *where* the boundary is located. He should get up after every play and look to see where the ball is spotted. He should be talking to himself on the way back to the huddle about down and distance. He must know what the other team likes to do in those situations. Then he must relay the information you have taught him to the other players in the huddle. The linebacker must communicate with the rest of the team.

There are some things that we use to grade our linebackers on to tell them if they had a good game or not. When I took the job at Notre Dame, Coach Holtz told me he did not care what defensive fronts we ran or what alignments we ran. The front or alignment you are in does not matter as far as winning and losing are concerned. But Coach Holtz did tell me he was looking for certain things in our defense. We grade our kids in the films on these points. First is what we call *pads out*. That is the explosion of our players. If we are absorbing the licks and not giving them out, then we grade them down. We want to give the licks.

Second is *shoulders square*. We want to see our entire defensive team playing with their shoulders square. It is especially true for the linebackers. When our linebackers shuffle from tackle to tackle, I want their feet in a good basic position. Naturally, when the ball gets outside we can't shuffle. But we can keep our shoulders square. A drill I use the first day of practice to emphasize keeping the shoulders square is a shuffle drill. The ballcarrier starts out walking. The linebacker gets on his hip and is down in a good football position. He shuffles to start out with. Then the coach tells him to jog. The linebacker continues to keep his position as he shuffles. Next, the coach tells the ballcarrier to run. Now the linebacker can no longer shuffle and keep up. He has to cross over and do whatever he can do, but he must keep his shoulders square. The drill is for 40 yards of walking and jogging and running.

The next point we look for is the headgear, pads, and hands. When the linebacker makes contact with a blocker, the blocker does not make contact with the meat of his body. When someone comes to block the linebacker, all they get is the head, hands, and shoulder pads. He has inside leverage and does not give the blocker any surface to block. The next point we grade our linebackers on is missed assignments. If the linebackers don't have the game plan down pat by Wednesday, we scratch the part that they do not know. They have to totally understand what we want by Wednesday or we are not going to use it. I would rather go into a game with one scheme, and play it right with no mental errors, than to go into a game with a great plan to stop everything, but the players do not understand it. If your opponent puts a bunch of points on the scoreboard, you can go back and check things out and you will find that you made a lot of mental errors. Squeeze the game plan down so the offense has to beat you. Don't beat yourself on defense.

Our offensive line coach at Notre Dame is Joe Moore. Joe coached at Pitt several years and just about everyone he worked with became All-Pro. One day, in a staff meeting, Coach Holtz told Joe, "Years ago you would have driven me crazy. You meet with your players less than any other coach. At times, you do not even talk to your players on the field. However, your players keep getting better and better. I do not understand it. Joe, you do not even communicate with them and they are getting better. How do you explain this?" Joe told Lou this story: "When I was a small kid, our family moved into a house that was only 12 feet from a train track. Between midnight and seven in the morning, three trains would go by our house. The trains would wake everyone up, and it was hard to get a good night's sleep. The first three weeks, I could not sleep at all. I decided to do something about it. I decided to pretend that the trains did not come by at all. I blocked them out of my mind. Then I couldn't hear the trains and I was able to sleep at night. I decided when I became a coach I was not going to be like a 'train' to the kids I work with." This story sounds simple, but it makes sense. If you are talking all of the time in practice, and the players are not getting the reps they need, they will not get better. If you talk all of the time, they will not hear what you are saying. When we are on the field, we talk as little as possible. We try to get across our point and get in as many reps as possible.

The next thing we grade our players on is penalties. We do not want any foolish penalties. We do not want them to spear, grab the face mask, or any other foolish thing like that. We tell them they are going to get some aggressive penalties, but we do not want any foolish penalties. The next thing we stress is pass rush lanes. We film from behind the quarterback in the passing game to show our defensive linemen. We want them to know what the quarterback sees from the pass rush. If our defensive linemen are in their proper pass rush lanes, the quarterback can't see his receivers. All the quarterback can see is defensive hands and arms and then he has to anticipate where his receivers are. As soon as the defensive linemen get out of their lane, it opens up an alley and a throwing lane for the quarterback. Our linemen can see this on the films. We want to make the quarterback throw out of the well. We want the quarterback to throw up and over the oncoming rushing linemen.

We do not want any ballcarrier falling forward. This goes back to keeping the shoulders square. We tell them to keep the playside arm and leg free. If they do not keep their outside arm and leg free, they get graded down. If they get blocked, they get graded down. It all goes back to missed assignments. They must keep the proper relationship with the blocker.

Next, we tell them to stay on their feet. Don't get cut down. If you stress keeping a wide base, you can go through a game and not get knocked down. You can get the players to develop great pride in keeping their feet, especially linebackers. Anytime a linebacker falls down, he gets a minus. It does not matter if his own man knocks him down; he gets a minus. A linebacker should not be on the ground. The linebacker has to play the cut block with his hips. If he plays it with his hands, he gets exposed. He is just like a wrestler. You bend your hips and the arms come out, your eyes go up, and you keep your feet away from the man. When the football is pitched, we want 11 people pressing the line of scrimmage, on their feet, running to that football with their shoulders square.

We teach our linebackers to go across the face. We do not want them to run around blocks. That is one of the most unnatural things in football. The natural thing to do is to take the easy way out against the block. That is the area of least resistance.

The next two points are involved with the secondary. We want *no passes or runs over 20 yards*. This relates to the secondary as well as the linebackers. Also, proper pursuit angles and how we chase the ball are important. The last thing we grade them on is hustle. We do not want them loafing. This is self-explanatory.

Those are the points we use to grade our players. All position coaches use these same points. After we play on Saturday, Coach Holtz wants to see our evaluation sheets in those areas. They are on his desk by Sunday at noon. He wants to know how the defensive team has done in those areas. The first thing he looks at is mental errors. The next thing he looks at is football position. Then he looks to see who loafed in the game. He can tell if we played a good game or not by looking at that grade sheet.

When I coached at Iowa, I had a linebacker who graded out 95 to 98 percent every game. He did everything right. But when we looked at the end results, in 60 plays he would only get one or two tackles and no assists. The man playing behind him would get seven or eight tackles, and force a fumble, but he only played in 10 plays. He would run around a block or make a mistake and end up grading out at about 75 percent. This made me think there was something wrong with the way we were grading our players. If that second linebacker could play 60 plays, we might get something done on defense. I decided to revise my grading system and came up with a bottom line grading system. This is what really counts as far as winning and losing is concerned. When the game is over, we can see who is productive. Every play was graded. If you did everything right, you got a plus. If you did something wrong, you got a minus. If you got a plus, you got one point. If you got a minus, you got zero points. Bonus points were awarded for assisted tackles, unassisted tackles, tipped passes, interceptions, fumble recovery, and causing a fumble. If you scored on defense, you got 10 points.

Let me give you a good example of this system. Let's take Mike Stonebreaker against Michigan State. He had 21 tackles, intercepted two passes (one for a touchdown), and he blocked a punt. He ended up with a 2.7 average. That is tremendously high. But, you can see that he was involved in a lot of big plays. If a linebacker averages 2.0, he has had a great game. We want the outside linebackers to grade out to 2.0. We want the defensive linemen to play good to average and grade out 1.5. The secondary will grade out lower than the rest of the defense. But, if you have a linebacker grading out at 1.1 or worse, he is not playing very well. I look at this first. A linebacker has to make plays. If he doesn't make plays, you are not going to be very good defensively.

I want to go back and talk on linebacker techniques. We call this *movement and blow*. I have told you that we want them to keep their shoulders square and to keep a good base with their feet. We always have them shuffle between the tackles. We do not want the feet to come together when they shuffle. The linebacker has to keep leverage on all plays. Most tackles are missed because of overrunning the ball or by closing the eyes. The linebacker has to press the line of scrimmage and not give the ballcarrier a cutback lane. He must take the angle that forces the back to cut back into his face. If the back goes for the boundary, the angle allows the linebacker to get his head across the ballcarrier and run him out of bounds. We use that boundary as a defender.

If the linebacker comes flat, and does not press the line of scrimmage, he gives the ballcarrier a cutback move. We tell them to attack the play— don't wait for the play to come to you. If the linebacker's gap is threatened, he attacks the gap. If the flow goes away and his gap is not threatened, he is to pursue and hug the heels of the defensive linemen. He must continually press the line of scrimmage. If he sees a seam and he has a reasonable chance to get to the ball, he runs through the seam. We want the minus yardage plays. We look for the run-through lanes to create those losses.

An area overlooked by many coaches is taking on blockers. I do not think coaches spend enough time working on these techniques. There are three different ways that you can take on blockers. Very seldom do we see a straight drive block anymore. Most of the time, it is zone blocking, where the linemen come off at an angle. Against the drive block, I have to get my pad under his pad and stop his momentum. We want to collision with our shoulder pad and at the same time get a snap in the hips to get separation. If you look at your films, you will not find the drive block used 10 times all year. Most of the time, we see the cutoff block. To combat the angle zone block, we teach an inside lift. We want the outside arm locked to keep separation. The inside arm lifts and punches into the blocker to keep him from turning and running downhill on the defender.

The third thing we teach is the shiver. As the linebacker attacks the line of scrimmage, he has to learn to punch with his inside arm to square his shoulders. We drill our players every day on this. They deliver blows on blockers. We teach our players how to protect themselves and to get off the blocker.

When we teach tackling, the first thing we teach is inside out on the ballcarrier. We use the sideline drill all season. We worked on this the first day we were in pads, and we did it three days before the Orange Bowl. We work on it all season. We go with our good players against the good offensive players. We set up along the sideline and give the ballcarrier about seven yards to run in. He can do anything he wants. The linebacker has to learn to press forward and keep the ballcarrier from cutting back. He presses and works the ballcarrier to the boundary. If the back cuts back, we tackle him. If he goes to the sideline, we get our head across the bow and force him out of bounds.

In tackling, the power comes from the hips. Every team has a little player who plays in the secondary. You see that little back come up and knock people flat when he tackles. Then you see a big 280-pound tackle who just pushes the back down when he tackles. The difference is in the explosion in the hips. When we tackle, we come off a one-foot takeoff. We like to angle tackle. We cock our hands, keep our head up, and tackle with our chest. Everything we do is an explosion and a club-up move. Once we make contact, we get our head across the bow and run through with the legs.

We have a basic rule in our pass coverage for the linebackers. They are responsible from tight end to tight end alignment. When they read pass, they are going to open their hips and run to the point over the tight end alignment. As they open their hips to run, they take a peak at the tight end. As they work back, their eyes never leave the quarterback. If the tight end runs straight down the field, the linebacker should have a collision with him at about 12 yards deep. That is the widest point in the linebacker's zone. Once the quarterback sets to throw, the linebacker sets up. He gets his shoulders square and starts to buzz. If the tight end works outside, the linebacker may go with him. That is the only way the linebacker would get more width. When the quarterback stops to throw, the linebacker chokes his motor down and gets set for the action. Anytime the ball is thrown deep, it has to go over a player's hands. If the quarterback throws the ball down the middle of the field 15 yards deep, we want one of our linebackers to tip the ball, or have it go over his hands.

We work on this in practice. We put a corner, two linebackers, and a strong safety in a four-under scheme. The coach simulates the quarterback. When he tilts his shoulders, all the underneath coverage shuffles in the direction of the tilt. We place four stationary receivers behind the coverage. The coach throws the ball to one of these four receivers and the defense breaks on the flight of the ball. The key is to break on the ball flat. If they do that, the ball will be thrown over the receiver's head, or the linebackers will tip the ball. If the quarterback can lay the ball over the linebackers in front of the safeties all day, you are in for a long day. The natural reaction is for the defenders to break back toward the receiver. When the defensive man breaks back to the receiver, it opens a passing lane for the ball to come through. The secondary coach can stand back about 12 yards to see the reaction of the defenders. All of them should be breaking flat on the ball. If any of them break back, that is where the passing lane will be.

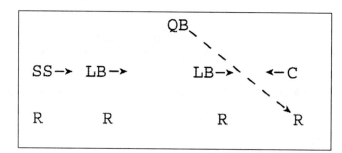

The linebackers have to study the routes a team runs. They can tell where to go by the routes the tight end runs. If the tight end runs flat, the linebacker gets width and looks for the number two man coming inside. If the tight end crosses, the linebacker sits and waits for someone to work back inside. If the tight end runs to get to the open area, the linebacker latches on him and fights him because he is threatening his zone. If the tight end runs a hook route, the linebacker gets inside leverage on him and looks to the quarterback.

To the open-end side of the formation, the linebacker is responsible for the number two receiver to that side. He plays the zone to that side as if there were a tight end to his side. When an I formation team gives us a sprint draw look, the backside linebacker's reaction is a little different. When he sees the tailback going to the strongside, he is going to react to that side. He reacts to that side and looks for the tight end. If he comes on the drag route, the linebacker works back and treats him as a number one receiver to that side. As the tight end continues to the flat, he gets into his zone and plays number two coming inside.

Our linebackers key the backs. I do not think you have to key linemen. If you play any defense where the guards are covered, you can't read fast enough or get a true enough read to play the way you need to play. When you take the scouting report, you will see that most teams only run about seven plays. They may throw a lot of bull crap at you, but 90 percent of the time they run seven or eight basic plays. Those seven or eight plays are what you cover with your defense.

When we line up at Wisconsin this spring, this is how we will look. We will be in what I call a split look. In our *split look*, we have a 9 and a 5 technique, and the nose

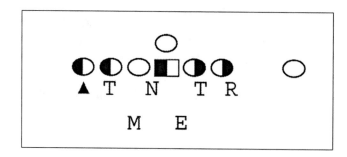

is in the 1 gap to the strongside. On the backside, we have a 3 and a 5 technique. The Mike linebacker is responsible for both his A and B gaps. The Eagle linebacker is responsible for his A gap.

We drill our defense on the basic plays we expect them to see in their area. Against the I formation, they can expect to see the sweep, isolation, counter, and the sprint draw. We teach them where to go, and who to expect to block them on each action. We can get 15 to 20 reps before practice by using the managers to walk through the plays for our linebackers. We set up cones or bags to show them their responsibilities and gaps, and then we make them react. From there, we go to our individual inside drills with the linemen. Finally, we get into the team drills where they can see the whole picture. We spend our time working against the basic plays we expect to see in the game. We do not spend a lot of time working on trick plays. You have to stop the plays that you are going to see for most of the game.

We tell our Eagle linebacker he is a 1-gap player. He has the backside 1 gap. If flow goes away with any threat of coming back inside, he goes into the 1 gap. The first play he looks for is the sprint draw. He goes into the 1 gap just like he is running a stunt. I want the ballcarrier to look up and see that every gap is filled. If the linebacker shuffles instead of filling, he gets into a lot of trouble. On flow toward the Eagle linebacker, he is free to go to the ball. If it goes outside, he goes to the alley on the quarterback.

On the split-back set, the linebackers key the inside legs of the backs. If the back goes lateral, they take one step with him and then check back to the inside, looking for the counter. As the linebacker steps lateral, he picks up the inside leg of the other back. Against the wishbone set, the linebackers key all three backs. They key *flow*. If we played a wing-T team, we probably would cross key with our linebackers. This stops the fullback trap, which is one of the best plays from that set.

Gentlemen, my time is up. I hope all of you are successful next year.

2

Linebacker Fundamentals and Techniques

Ron Burton
Indiana University
1999

I want to give you a little bit about my background so you will know where I am coming from. I am originally from Virginia. I went to North Carolina, where I got a chance to play and coach. I know that as coaches, we are interested in our kids doing their best. I got that same feeling when I was in high school. My coach felt as though he was not working, he was coaching. He was doing something he loved to do.

As I said, I went to North Carolina, where I got a chance to play for Dick Crum. From North Carolina, I went to the NFL. I got a chance to play as a free-agent rookie. I was one of 150 free agents. I went out with the Dallas Cowboys. I got a chance to see Tom Landry in action. That planted the seed that I wanted to coach. I got to see Tom Landry. Then came a guy named Jimmy Johnson. I got to see another coaching style. He believed that if you could not make the play, you should not be with the Cowboys. A few games into the season, I was cut, but I learned a lot from those experiences. I did go on to play for Gene Stallings and the Phoenix Cardinals. I finished my NFL career with Art Shell and the Raiders. Again, all of this was validation that I wanted to be a coach. You are what you experience, and you are what you are around. It was a great start for me. I have been blessed. I am 35 years old; some people think that is young, and some people think that is old. My experiences as a player helped me to become a coach. I use those experiences with my players every day.

I even use my experience with my four kids every day. I have three boys and a girl. I am always trying to get them to do their best. I do the same thing with them as I do with my players. I know that I am dealing with 18- and 19-year-old kids and I have to stay as simple as possible. I have tried to create something today that will help you.

I am going to talk about the basic fundamentals of linebackers. At Indiana, we are dealing with a lot of young kids because we are in a transition period in our program. We try to do everything possible to make those kids train themselves to bend their knees and to play hard.

All of the things I am going to go over here are things I have accumulated over the years. We use the KISS principle at Indiana: Keep It Simple, Stupid! We are going to talk about the fundamentals.

First is our philosophy. Our philosophy is to execute the basic fundamentals and techniques that put your body in the best position to make plays by focusing and finishing what you are doing. That is the first thing you will see in our playbook.

Next, we talk about the qualities required to be a great linebacker. We list five things that are required:

- Leadership—recognition and communication (early and often)
- Savvy, alertness, instinct—diagnose situations
- Physical toughness, attack BF, pulling guards
- Quick violent reactor, speed to run down spills
- Speed, agility, quickness

I give my players a term to go look up once a week or once a day. We stress focus: to concentrate and to produce a clear mental image. What does focus mean? Some players have a short attention span. Let them know what it takes to get the job done or what it takes to play this position. You must focus on what is to be taught. What are the responsibilities, and what do they do? Then you have to focus on how. They must learn the techniques to carry out assignments. We want them to play aggressively and to physically get the job done.

Every linebacker must know the four mental and physical techniques to be successful. These are things we give them in our KISS package. We harp on this all of the time.

Mental Techniques

- Communication—It happens from the beginning of the play to the end of the play. It comes from the press box down to the coach on the sideline, to the player, and back to the coach. They have to understand that. We want our kids to talk as much as possible.
- Alignment

- Key—We put them in position to focus on their key. This is discipline. We have to build on this with young players.

- Assignment, adjustment, stance

Physical Techniques

- Tackling—Tackling is a desire. We will talk about that.

- Hit and shed—Being able to get to a block and then to get off the block.

- Pursuit—How do you get there? There are all types of pursuits.

- Zone techniques—We used a lot of zone coverages this past year. We ended up second in the Big 10 and third in the nation in turnover ratio.

The first thing we talk about is our stance. These are the points we stress on our stance:

- The feet must be slightly wider than armpits' width apart. Some people say shoulders' width, but the shoulders are outside, and for some players that is too wide.

- Toes pointed straight forward at the line of scrimmage.

- Weight of body on toes and balls of feet, heels on the ground.

- Knees bent slightly past the front of the feet. The knees are flexing over the toes.

- Legs tense, ready for sudden movement. Be ready to react.

- Bend forward at the waist, head and chest slightly past the knees. We want the weight forward.

- Hands outside knees with palms facing inward or parallel to legs.

- Bulled neck; eyes up on target or key. Get in a position to see through to your key.

- Upper body relaxed in order to move freely, tensing only before contact. We do that because it allows us to move in a fluid manner before getting into position to make a play.

We want our kids to understand the overall progression of teaching. We sugarcoat it for them. Fundamentals: PASKAT!

Presnap: Communication.

Alignment: Rules, shades, and deportment.

Stance and start: Football position.

Key: Focus eyes. Progression, discipline.

Assignment: Know and execute, run or pass.

Technique: Football position, eyes under, square to the line of scrimmage.

This is just something for the kids to hang on to. It is P-A-S-K-A-T. They can understand it and relate to it.

I think the most important thing a linebacker does is tackling. We talk about tackling fundamentals. Someone said that tackling is desire. You can find guys who just love contact. They find a way to make the tackle. We start with desire in tackling.

Desire

- Focus and hat placement—Focus on the jersey numbers, eyes, and tips of the ball. This is just before contact.
- Base—Body weight is ahead or out in front of his base. It is all body control. You should do anything to teach the kids to control their bodies.
- Explosion of hips and arms—Body control is the key. We want to put ourselves in the best position to explode up through the man.
- Down the football—We just want the ball on the ground. Tackle the football. Remember, there is no perfect tackling. I will show you every tackle we make. There is no perfect tackle.

We will talk about the type of tackling we practice. I will cover these later.

- Form tackling
- Sweep tackle
- Square tackle
- Eye-opener

The most important thing a linebacker has to do is to tackle. How do you find out if they can tackle? You put them out there and turn them loose. We will find the guy who loves to run down the football.

Next is the hit-and-shed technique. We talk about hitting and shedding. It starts with your foundation.

Hit-and-Shed Base

Correct base (feet)—What is the correct base? When your feet are in total relationship and slightly forward, with your shoulder over the lead foot. Two no-no's that we see: First is the opposite foot and shoulder base. The second is the pancake base. They never get the lead foot in the ground prior to contact.

Pad level—This is what we concentrate on. My pad is under his pad. If my pad is under his pad, we have a better chance of shedding the blocker.

Hip roll or explosion—You can explode the hips up and through the man. This puts you in the best position to attack.

Upper body—If you have a correct base with the feet, have the pads level, and have hip explosion, you are in the best position to take on blockers. We teach face and hands. We get kids from high school who have not learned to use their hands. We teach them to do anything they can to stay on balance to ward off a blocker. We want them to use the hands with the thumbs up and the palms out. We want them to use the hard joints with the shoulder. We teach them to use the elbow flipper.

I will show you our drills later in the film. One drill we use to warm up is our shuffle shed drill.

Shuffle Shed Drill

Description:

- Hitting position in front of cone.

- Start with quicker jag step at 45 degrees.

- Shuffle up into the line-of-scrimmage bags.

- Pads down; hands and head up!

- Jam with hands and shoulder; use face and hand technique.

- Continue to shuffle two more times.

- Turn; accelerate to ballcarrier or cone.

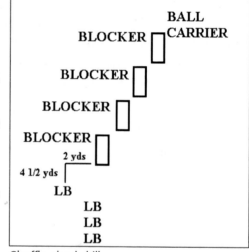
Shuffle shed drill

Points of Emphasis: Do not stop in between bags. Do not stop feet. Stay on the move. Keep pad level low. Check pad level by blocker's pads; linebacker's helmet needs to be lower than blocker.

Now I want to talk about pursuit. We define pursuit as the act of following so as to overtake or capture. The first move we teach is the shuffle. It is a controlled movement used parallel to the line of scrimmage when the ball is moving slowly, usually in a high-contact area. We are moving in the area from tackle to tackle.

Coaching Points:

- Stay square (for C.O.D., or change of direction).
- Slide your feet (never cross over).
- Stay low (bend at the hips).
- Maintain vision (to maintain proximity to runner). Know what is going on.

That was a particular pursuit, the shuffle. The next tackle pursuit we call *alley*. Alley is when you turn your *hips*, cross over, and run inside out on the ball. We work the arms hard to keep the *shoulders square*, usually in low-contact areas. We want to maintain a three-yard cushion to adjust in open field. During pursuit, your attitude should be, "Please cut back." Never be surprised by a cutback run!

Coaching Points:

- You must work the arms hard to keep shoulders square.
- Maintain three-yard cushion.
- Expect the cutback runs.
- Expect crack-back and cut blocks.

We want to press vertically, attacking the line of scrimmage downhill. The longest running plays in football are cutbacks or runs that break behind the backside linebacker.

Pursuit Drills—Cone and Box

Cone Drill: Ready to position, shuffle, alley, press.

Box Drill: Shuffle, press, alley, press, shuffle, backpedal, alley.

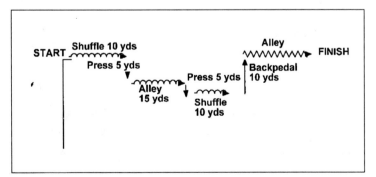

Pursuit drills

Next, I want to talk about the fundamentals of pass defense. First is our philosophy. The second part of the linebackers' responsibilities is to help stop the pass. When pass is recognized, the linebacker becomes either a rush man or part of the secondary as a pass defender. The success of the pass defense will, to a large extent, depend on how well the linebackers play their underneath coverages. When a pass has been diagnosed, the linebacker must know and understand what to do with his eyes, brains, and body. A lot of concentrated practice is the only way we will become proficient in defending the passing game.

Three Basic Coverage Points

Stance—The linebacker's stance will basically remain the same, but his alignment may loosen or widen, depending on the coverage called and the opponent's formation.

Key—For the most part, the run and pass key will remain the same, but depending on the coverage called, the linebacker's keys could change with the snap of the ball.

Drops—After diagnosing pass, time is of the essence in getting control of the man coverage or into the zone area.

Factors That Affect the Drop

Man-to-Man

- Any deep help
- Inside or outside help
- Field position (yard line or hash)

Zone Coverage

- Area to be covered
- Hash marks and sideline
- Quarterback action
- Down-and-distance

Everyone knows what zone coverage is, but we will review it anyway. What is a zone defense? It is a designated area that a linebacker has to cover that is between the line of scrimmage and the secondary. You are covering an area, but you have to be aware of receivers in your area.

I tell our kids to take home their playbook. They can use the playbook to learn a lot of these techniques. They need to get a bell captain in the off-season. That is a man who knows what he is doing. Get them out and let them be a coach.

Techniques That Are Necessary: Keys

- Recognize the pass by making sure the quarterback clears the running backs before bursting to a proper depth of 12 to 15 yards in the zone.

- Turn and run laterally, looking over the shoulder at the quarterback.

- As you are going to your zone, glance for receivers coming into your zone, never taking your eyes completely off the ball. Be able to react quickly to the quarterback's throw through your area to another.

- Always position yourself between the ball and the receivers in zone, being able to break down to football position within three yards off the receiver and out of your peripheral vision.

- Break at an angle to react and intercept the ball. If a receiver breaks inside, pivot back to react to the ball.

- If no receiver is in the zone at 12 to 15 yards deep, then square your shoulders to the line of scrimmage, with weight on the balls of your feet in a slow backpedal and the elbows close to the body, looking for the receiver.

- React to all looks of the quarterback, communicating any crossing routes to the other defenders.

One drill we use is the bag 45s. This is what it looks like. This is one of my favorite drills.

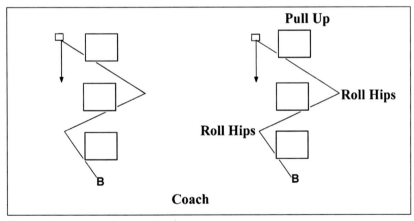

Bag 45s

Bag 45s

Description:

- Open up at 45 degrees.

- They must see the quarterback and peripheral receiver.

- The coach is the quarterback. He directs the linebacker through the minefield of bags. The bags are five yards apart. He points the ball left or right.

- At any point, the coach can step up to throw. The linebacker must focus on the coach.

- The linebacker must pull up and break on the ball.

I want to show you the film of our drills. If you have something that you want to question, feel free to ask. In the tape, you will see some good plays, and you will see some bad plays. You will see some tackles and say, "That is a bad tackle. Where is the ballcarrier? He is on the ground." Seldom do you see the perfect tackle. Football is not like that.

We do a lot of drills. I tell our kids that we will not do any drill that does not show up in the game films. I have these drills on tape. If you want a copy, call me up, and I will get it done for you. If there is anything we can do for you, let me know.

Guys, we are what we say we are. Teach your kids. Let them know that this is important to them. What you do with your kids allows them to be a product of their environment. Make sure your kids take something from you. God bless you.

3

Linebackers in the Oklahoma Defense

Gary Gibbs
University of Oklahoma
1991

The thing I like about our defensive staff at Oklahoma is the fact that we are always looking for a better way to do things. It is not an "I" concept with us. We do not have one coach dictating everything to our defensive staff. We have a defensive coordinator that leads the group, but he does not dominate the group. We work very well together on defense. We work together as a unit. That is the key to coaching and that is the fun part of coaching. We are in the process of analyzing our defensive package to see if we can make it better. We evaluate our personnel to see if they are in the right position. Also, we want to look at our techniques and determine if our players are playing the right techniques. We have a lot of people back, but we know we cannot sit back and just think we will have a great team without working to get better.

Some of you may know that we have been on probation for two years. In 1989, we were not on national TV. However, we were able to appear on TV last year five times. I am bringing this up because we have changed our offensive thinking somewhat in that time period. We are no longer just simply a wishbone football team. We are an option team, but we are throwing the football. We are not just throwing the ball in practice; we are throwing the ball in the games. That has helped our offense a great deal. We have a quarterback that is very exciting and can throw the football.

When we were a wishbone football team, we were a tough team. You practice against that wishbone every day. You have to be tough to endure. We were a tough defensive football team mainly because of the competition against our own wishbone.

Conversely, our defensive secondary would see very few passes in practice when we ran the wishbone. As a result, our secondary got very little practice against the pass. When we played good passing teams like UCLA and Miami, we were at a big disadvantage. Now, I think the change in direction we are taking, offensively, will help us a great deal on defense. It has helped our defensive staff in getting our defense ready to play.

I want to talk primarily about our eagle linebacker play. The thing we tell our coaches about our defense is this: This is not a complex equation. We are not talking about physics or chemistry. We tell our coaches to find the best linebackers they can find, and then tell them, "Sic 'em." Our basic defense is an eagle package. Some people call it a *split eagle*. Some people may call it a *35 look*. Others may call it a *53 look*. This is what our basic front looks like.

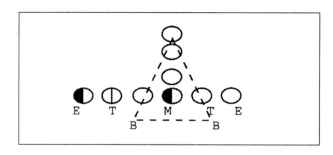

We play with three down linemen. We have two stand-up ends and linebackers. We feel this gives us a lot of speed and quickness with four people in a standing-up position. Some other teams are playing this same defense, in college and in the pros. The difference is that they have the end on the split end side down in a four-point stance. He is not a true stand-up or drop player. That is a four down linemen concept. We play a three down linemen concept. The reason we are playing the three down linemen is because we have a hard time finding four tough, hard-charging down linemen. We feel we have more flexibility in pass coverage with an end that is in a stand-up position. We feel the ends and linebackers are the key to our defense. When we have had great linebackers at Oklahoma, we have had good defense. They have to be the playmakers or quarterbacks on defense for us. They have to make all of the checks and adjustments. They have to make things happen for us. I am not interested in the linebacker that makes 20 tackles per game, but is always dragging down the backs after they make three or four yards on each play. We want the linebacker that can make the big play. We are looking for guys that can make the negative play or the big play.

Our linebackers are going to line up a shade to the outside of the offensive guards. We line them up three-and-a-half yards from the line of scrimmage. This is a change-up for us from what we used to play. Before, we would play up on the heels of our defensive tackles, when we had linebackers like Brian Bosworth. When you are playing a team like Nebraska, which is an assault type team, you have to play tight to the line to get to them.

Our basic stance is squared up. We do allow them to stagger their feet a little, if they want. The thing is that we want them to have quick feet. We do not like to play our linebackers five yards deep, but we do want them at three-and-a-half yards. We do not want them to cross their feet. We want them to have good feet, and have a feel for the ball.

Our key is the fullback. We key through the guard to the fullback. Our initial movement against an I back set is to key the fullback and feel the I back in the deep I set. We want to feel the tailback and the quarterback. The good linebackers can do this. If they can't, you should make them put their hand on the ground and play as a down lineman. If the linebackers can't feel the tailback and quarterback, they do not need to be playing linebacker. They have to have some instincts. The advantage of this defensive front is that it frees the linebackers up so they can make the tackles. The Will linebacker does not have to sit in there and take on those big blocking guards all day long. We do not expect our linebackers to sit inside and take on the guards all day. The shade nose has the responsibility to fill the 1 gap. He wants to put pressure on the center so he can't make a cutoff block against the Sam linebacker. If the ball goes away from the noseguard, he has to keep the center off the backside linebacker. The linebackers can get away from the tackles and guards if the nose man will give us some help. We look for the linebackers that can run.

Our defensive line technique is critical to our overall linebacker play. We want to make sure we are jamming the offensive linemen. We want to disrupt the linemen on their release. We do not want the offensive linemen taking an easy cutoff release. This allows him to get down inside on our linebackers. If our defensive linemen are not willing to jam the offensive line, and be physical with them, then we will find someone else that will. We do not want our down linemen making the plays on defense. Our key is for our inside linebacker and our two outside people to make the tackles.

We used to stagger our stance for our down linemen. They would put that inside hand down, and on the snap of the ball they would take that inside hand and move it on the ball, trying to move the inside foot to the spot where the hand was on the ground. We are changing this next year. We used to see base blocks against us. We do not see the base block anymore. Everyone is using the zone block, or area block, or cutoff blocks. We are still going to stagger our stance some, but we are not going to be as aggressive as we used to be on the line of scrimmage. We are going to go to what some of the pro teams are doing, and what some high school teams are doing. We are going to be more of a "mirror" type team. We want to mirror the offensive linemen moves. We feel this will give our linemen more power. This should give us a better strength base. Hopefully, this will allow us to get to the ball a little quicker. Our tackles play a 5 or 4 technique. If they are in a tight stance, they can get cut off a lot easier up on the man.

We do all the warm-up types of things that you do. After we stretch, we run our key drill. We do this drill every day. After the offense breaks the formation, we break our defensive set. Then we recognize the formation, and recognize the backfield set. The next thing we do is to believe what that backfield set is telling us. *We teach our linebackers to read the play as it develops.* Let me show you what I am talking about.

Anytime we get the fullback moving in the direction of the two linebackers, we call that a *north* or a *south trap path.* We tell the linebacker this: "If he comes—you come." When that fullback comes north or south, we attack. We talk about the path of the fullback, and determine how he is going to play. We talk in terms of path and play. "If the path of the fullback is this, it will be this play. If the path of the fullback is this, it will be another play. Based on that path, and based on the recognition of the play, *this is how we want to play."* We go and attack the fullback on his north-south path.

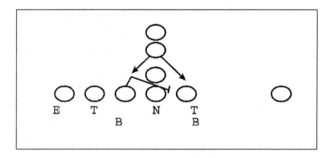

We see this type of play from teams like Nebraska, or other teams that play the I formation. We see the play to our eagle side, or away from the shade noseguard. As our Will linebacker reads the fullback coming toward him, he steps up and accelerates and looks for the guard. We see the play blocked two ways. One way is with the guard pulling around to trap the Will linebacker. When I see the guard on the trap, I want to take him on with my long arm. I want to rip through the guard with my outside arm and force the ball to bounce to my 3 technique. I do not want to take on the guard with my inside arm and take a chance of getting trapped outside. That could let the fullback get into the end zone in a flash. I want to long-arm the pulling guard and force the ball to our 3 technique.

If the offense traps our 3 technique, we must beat the fullback coming straight ahead. If the tackle tries to get inside of the pulling guard, the linebacker must step up and get inside the tackle's block. He can do that if he is reading the fullback's path. The thing we do not want is for that fullback to maintain his north-south trap path. We do not get much help from our defensive end on the jam against the tackle and guard. The main thing is to get that fullback off his north-south path. We have stunts to help us with this. We can send that 3 technique into the defensive tackle. That takes the edge off the tackle. This allows the Will linebacker to step up and take on the fullback. They do not call that play many more times after that. If you are a great trapping team, we will play stunts.

Where we get hurt on this set is the trap option. This gives us more problems. We see the freeze option some, and we see it in the spring against our own team. If we do see a trap play to the 5 technique side, which we all see, the key is the nearside linebacker. He steps up and reads the fullback. He has to get inside the block. If we are playing against a split back set, the linebacker keys the near back on his side. We see the I set or the power I set the most.

The next path we talk about in our key drill is the *dive path*. The fullback takes an aiming point on the outside hip of the guard. We want our linebacker to read that path and get the feel for the play. We feel the shade noseguard must beat the tackle on this play. We do not feel our tackle will be reached on the outside shade. The center is at a disadvantage against the shade guard. He cannot be reached. We want the Sam linebacker to press the 3 gap. He must get into the dive path on the play. We want him to dip and rip. We want him to close off the 3 gap and force the ball to go somewhere else. We do not want the Sam linebacker to play lateral. We do not want him to catch the guard. We want him to *dip* and *rip*. We want the linebacker to give the guard very little room with the shoulder pad on the dip Then we want him to rip up and press his body through the offensive guard through the 3 gap and force the ball to go somewhere else. Option football teams like to run the dive option. Wishbone teams used to run this play a lot of times. With the offset noseguard, you do not see it as much now. That is hard to block. It is tough to run that ball in the 3 gap.

Off the dive path is the isolation path. The Will back sees this a lot. When he sees the isolation path of the fullback, Will goes for the fullback as soon as he recognizes the isolation. We want to meet him on his side of the ball. "He comes—I go." On the dive play, the quarterback works away from the center. That is a simple read for the linebacker. On the isolation play, the quarterback works behind the center. It is hard to defend because of the quarterback action. That is much harder for the linebacker to get the feel for the ball. Colorado, USC, and Nebraska know how to run that play. Years ago, that used to be a hard play to stop. A lot of teams have stopped running that play. I still think it is one of the real hard plays to stop in football. They would run to the eagle side, away from the noseguard. It is tough to stop if everything is equal.

What we have done is this: In the old days, we would take on the fullback with the inside shoulder and force the play back to the backside linebacker. We want to get a good jump ball and beat the fullback's block across the line of scrimmage. Now, with the combination blocks with the center and guard, teams are blocking the noseguard with one man, and have one man free to come off on the linebacker. This has forced us to change the way we play our frontside linebacker. We do not take the fullback on with the inside shoulder all of the time now. We will give our linebacker certain calls that have him taking on the linebacker more with his outside shoulder. He will try to force him outside our 3 technique to the 5 technique. This is a change-up to keep us from taking on that play the same way down after down.

The linebacker has to get a feel for the play. It is just like the trap play. That linebacker has to have a feel for what the quarterback is doing. They have to be conscious of the quarterback, regardless of the play.

We get our scout team and get two units of linebackers and work on our keys. If we are getting ready to play Nebraska, we will work on the dive and trap path. We work on our keys. We want to make sure our linebackers do not cross over, keep their shoulders square, and press the line of scrimmage. This is a key reaction drill, or play recognition without having to take on a bunch of blockers. If our linebackers can't read plays, they can't play for us. If they can read plays and diagnose plays, and have good feet and good quickness, they can play for us.

Next is our off tackle path. Now the fullback is blocking inside out. The aiming point of the fullback is the outside to inside hip of the offensive tackle. When the Sam linebacker recognizes the off tackle path, he wants to get tight and press the line of scrimmage as close as possible. He wants to come off the butt of the tight end. Now the quarterback is leaving the center and taking the ball to the tailback on the off tackle play. The fullback is working inside out on the end. The Sam linebacker is going to stay inside as long as he can. He does not want to get outside and cut himself off from the play. If he takes a false step, a crossover step, or overruns the play, it is the same as if he were blocked. We want our linebacker over the tight end—not where he lines up, but where he is going to be when the ball gets there. We do not want to get flushed outside with the pulling guard. We need to be off the tail of the tight end.

Our basic technique with our defensive end is to take on the blocker with our inside shoulder. We want to force the ball back to the inside. We want to force the offensive guard to make the tackle as we jam him into his running back. We may change up our basic pass coverage and that would make a difference how we play our linebackers. If we are playing a lot of two deep, we do not want the ball to get outside, wide. In pro football, most teams want to see the ball bounce outside. I want to see the ball bounce inside, where our noseguard and inside linebacker are free and have a chance to make the play. We are not going to bounce the play outside.

The key point here is to get off the butt of the tight end. The other key point is the Will linebacker. When he saw the dive path, the fullback still had a chance to cut back behind the noseguard. The Will linebacker has to be aware of the cutback.

The play that has given so many people trouble is the counter sweep, or counter trey play. Nebraska was the first team to run this play consistently. They ran this play in the early 1980's. They made a living with this play. This is the type of play that you have to stop with repetition. The more the linebackers see the play, the better they can recognize what is taking place. We key the fullback, but we still want to feel the quarterback and the tailback. Nowadays, not only do you have to defend the tailback counter, but what else? The tailback counter pass! That is right. The linebacker must get inside the fullback. The fullback will get inside on the defensive tackle to keep him from getting inside to the play. The fullback will go inside out. The quarterback is working directly behind the center. If the quarterback is working directly behind the center, we must defend against the misdirection. This is what we tell our linebackers. We have a summer high school football camp and we tell them the same thing in the camp. "Fullback starts, I start. When I feel the quarterback and tailback starting out, I retrace my steps and play just like I do on the off tackle play." I want the linebacker to retrace his steps and avoid all that garbage coming outside in. We tell our linebackers this: "If you choose to run through, you must make the play. The best thing is: start, retrace, and play it like an off tackle play." We want them to be physical with the offense in the running lane as soon as possible.

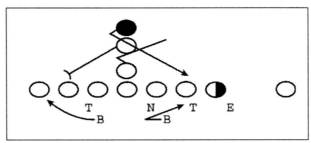

Everything is the same on the tailback counter pass except the fullback. The fullback is going to try to get outside of the defensive end and pin him down inside. The fullback runs inside out on the run, and outside in on the pass. It is hard to pick up on the videotapes. You run the tape back and stop it after the fullback takes one or two steps, and ask the linebacker, "Run or pass? What is the play? What is the play?"

We see several different sweep plays. Basically, against the sweep, we want to press and attack the line of scrimmage. If the guard pulls and the fullback is filling inside, we want to attack the fullback. Our tackle is in a 5 technique. The guard pulls and this gives us an alley for the Sam linebacker to run through. Sam wants to run through the alley at an angle. He wants to take on the fullback and force the tailback to change his path. If the linebacker can beat the fullback and make the tackle, that is great. If he can't, he wants to force the tailback off his path. He wants to make something happen that will help us on the play. We do not want to just sacrifice a linebacker one on one.

I have five minutes left for a few questions.

Question: How do you play the one back set?

Answer: Our basic adjustment is to move the inside linebacker outside on one of the split inside men. We are seeing teams that are not deploying their tailback or fullback on the one-back set, so we may not be in the eagle package against the trip set. We may bring in a fifth defensive back on the one-back set. If we can stay in our eagle package, we will adjust with our ends and linebackers.

Question: Do you play a lot of field defense?

Answer: We played some field defense a few years ago, before we went to a lot of substitutions on our defense. We have a lot of ability to make adjustments in the game with our defense on the field or we can make substitutions according to the offense. Against two tight ends, we may play two 4 techniques a lot. We may play two 4 techniques against the likes of Nebraska, because of their option and sweep game, as opposed to our eagle package. If we have to make an adjustment, our secondary has to be a part of the changes. On pass coverage, we are primarily a zone coverage team. We cover the passing zones the same way most of you do. The strongside linebacker has the tight end area. The Will linebacker has the curl area. We do not go to spots and tell our linebackers to read. We tell our Will linebacker an initial aiming point to help him. This helps him to know how far we want him to cover. It is a good coaching point.

Question: What techniques do you use on the tight end across?

Answer: If the tight end is playing off the linebacker, we tell him this: "If you have to step up to hit him, let him go." This is when we are at normal depth. The key words are "open up" and "hinge." If the end is shallow in front of the linebacker, he lets him go and looks for the area behind him. If the end is working off the linebacker, we do not want him to get across the field.

I have enjoyed this experience. You are welcome to come to Oklahoma to visit with us. We are an option team that is throwing the football. We are an eagle package team on defense. You are welcome to come visit with us. Thanks a lot.

4

Linebacker and End Techniques

John Guy
University of Kentucky
1991

Let me start by thanking everyone for being here this morning. I want to thank all the people I work with for the support they have given me over the years. I am what I am today because of a lot of people believing in me, and because of the work ethic that I have developed over the years working with a lot of good people. I feel the state of Kentucky is going to lose a great football mind and a great person when Rick Lantz goes to Virginia. He was very instrumental in my formative years of coaching.

I will talk about the play of the outside linebackers in the University of Kentucky package. A lot of people will tell you that the people I coach are not really linebackers. I will not argue with you on that, but at the University of Kentucky we call them *outside linebackers*. I will talk about the strike and the end on our multiple defense. They could be called ends in some defenses.

The way I want to conduct this talk is to take you through a series of things that I feel will help you understand our defense. I want you to feel free to stop me and ask questions at any time. I will try to give you the answers to the most common questions that I am asked about our defense, related to our strike and end.

To build on what Larry New talked about, I want to cover the play of the two men that I work with, the strike and the end position. Let me give you the job description for each. I call these two positions *half-man and half-animal*. These are the type of players that usually play these two positions. Over the years, they have been the type of players that live on the edge, and, in general, are kind of wild men. They do not have to be 6'4" and 245 pounds to play these positions. We have played men that were 6'2" and 225 pounds at these positions. What they do have to have is the ability to bend their knees and ankles. They must have good upper body strength, but they do not have to bench press 400 pounds. However, anything over 325 is considered good for them, and 385 is great. They have to be able to make decisions. I learned a long time ago that great players overcome coaching. These two players have to make decisions. They have to make great decisions. In football, you get beat on the perimeter and with the bombs. We have to be able to contain the offense or put pressure on them.

Players that play these two positions must be able to make plays in the off tackle area. If he can stay on his feet, and if he can make decisions, and has upper body strength, he can play these positions. In our scheme, we want to find the player that can make good decisions. We like players that have long arms playing these two positions. They must be able to use their hands on defense to play these two techniques.

The difference between the two is this: the strike sets our defense. In our scheme, the strike, tackle, Mike, and bandit all go together, right or left. The nose, end, and the Will go to the opposite side of the ball. The strike sets our defense. Another difference in the end and strike is this: the end is usually a little heavier. He has more alignments and is more of a technique player. He must be a very dependable player, because, a lot of times, he is over on the end by himself. The strike needs to be a little more agile and a quicker player, and a better change-of-direction player. He has to be a player that is willing to take a chance and be wrong at times.

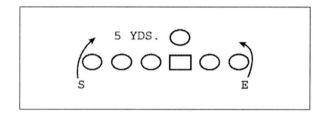

In my experience, I have found that players practice differently than they play. Players tend to think that they will play a lot better when they get in the game. They think they can play a lot better than they practice. What I do is this: I try to tee a player off early in practice to raise his level of performance to the same level he will play at during the game. A player will not do this on his own. I want them to raise their level of intensity from the beginning of practice all the way through the end of practice. I work hard on each player to try to find out what makes each player get to that point of intensity that he plays at in a game. You have to work at this for each player.

Two things that we feel get you in trouble on defense are your eyes and your feet. There are two other things that you need and they are correct hand and head placement. Let me comment a little about the eyes. We have found that football players tend to *stare*, rather than see through things. If we tell a player his key is a tight end, they will stare at the tight end and they will not see anything else. If you tell them their key is the back, they will stare at the back and they will not see anything else. The second thing that football players do is this: Football players tend to have a bond between each other, even with the opponents. If a defensive player is going to rush the passer, and rushes from the outside at some point, he is going to face the blocker. It may be a back in the backfield that he has to attack. Somewhere along that path, the two may look each other in the eye and know that they are going to go at it, one on one, on that play. They agree to make contact; it is just a natural thing. If the back is going to cut the defender, they both know that at some point, place, and time, they will say that it is just going to be "you and me." That is what happens to many football players. But the good players, they say, "Yes, let's get it on," and then they trick the blocker. There is that bond between football players, teammates, and opponents alike.

Let's talk more about the eyes of the strike and end. You have to see more than one thing. Let me give you an example by going over one technique. I think this is the toughest technique in our system. We have an alignment for the strike that is called *cinch*. For the end, it is called *tough*. The two have the same techniques, but we call them different terms. We are trying to coach eyes and feet. I always try to coach eyes and feet. If you put a special stripe on the player's helmet, you can see where the players are looking from the film.

In the cinch technique, we are going to key the tackle. We are going to look through the tackle, to the near back, pulling guard, quarterback, and whatever appears next. He must step at the tight end. He wants to make contact with the helmet and hands. He must step at the end and not laterally. He must drive the end back. Most players want to step laterally, and that is a mistake. The most passive position to play is in the parallel stance. If a player is in a parallel stance, he is getting ready to get his ass kicked, for the most part, or he is going to catch it from the offense. I think you need to be in a staggered stance to make the offense think you are coming hard. The stagger stance is much more aggressive on defense for the strike and end.

Let me comment on head placement. When you strike a blow, you need to strike through your eyebrows. Keep the head up, and look the lick in, through your eyebrows. That will keep your head up. Running backs run away from the opposite-color jersey or helmet. If they see the helmet is inside, they are going outside; if our helmet is outside, they go inside. It may be the jersey or the helmet, but running backs go opposite in most cases. On defense, we must aim our eyes and aim our head. If the tight end has a stripe or school logo on his helmet, that is to our advantage. I like for our defenders to key on that helmet stripe or logo. If that stripe goes parallel to the line of scrimmage, the tight end is probably going to arc release. If the stripe comes off at an angle, he is going to try to reach block the strike or end. We are still talking about head placement. The offense cannot get his helmet around you and hook you. The man can get the helmet outside, but you cannot let him get his body turned outside.

I want to talk about the pass rush. There are three basic kinds of pass rush. First is the *called pass rush*. This is where you tell your players to get down in a three-point stance and to come straight up the field. They know they have to rush. Second is the pass rush when you are in the base defense and nothing will tell the man to rush the passer. He must react to the passer. The third rush is the pass rush from a stunt. Let me talk about these three rushes.

First is the called rush. You have a call that has the strike rushing. If we have a called rush, we do not care if the offense knows we are coming. We put him in a three-point stance. To us, this is our "sooie" or "scream" stance. If we want all four front men rushing, we call, "Scream." If we call, "Sooie," it means we only send the end and strike. Those are our trigger terms. We want to get down in a three-point stance and get our butts up a little and turn loose. We want to run like we run a 40-yard dash. We try to give him some directions as to what he needs to know on each call. On a scream or sooie, we are trying to make that defensive man get deep. We want to make the blocker worry about beating him up the field perpendicular to the line of scrimmage. We want to get upfield five yards. If we can get the tackle to think we are going to beat him up the field, we have him on the run.

I have been very fortunate to work with some great pass rushers that had great desire in my coaching career. I have learned one thing about this technique. For a defensive man to get back five yards to sack the quarterback, it takes a great effort. You can make the call all you want, but if the rusher does not have the desire to get there, he won't. My style of coaching may be different than most coaches. Coaches can get caught up in trying to get the players to do as they say. I do not have a problem with a player in practice trying out what he can do, and what he can't do. But, to get to that point, he must prove to me that he can at least do what I ask him to do. Then I will let him experiment. If he can do that, then he deserves his chance to try something new.

The pass rush that we use to go with this call is our "bear in and lean" technique. That came from the Miami Dolphins. We are trying to beat the man up the field, and turn his shoulder pads and feet perpendicular to the line of scrimmage. As he turns, we want to take our inside shoulder pad and explode up and under the outside armpit. I do not like to use the rip technique. We do not want to get crossed in the move upfield. We want to throw our eyes to the sky and lift the arm off our neck. You must lean into the man and come up hard on the move.

If we have a man coming from the outside hard, we do not like to tell him to contain. On sooie, you let him go or you will not get any rush. This is a big rush for us.

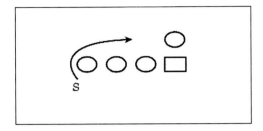

The next rush we get into is when we are in a base defense. For us, it could be 31 or 13. When we are talking about the three-man side, we are talking about the guard, tackle, and end. If we are talking about the two-man side, we are talking about the guard and tackle. On our base call, nothing is told to our end or strike to get upfield. They know in the base defense they must be a contain rusher. Before they can get upfield, they must do two things. First, they must see the tackle sit back quick, and the guard set back. Usually, you can tell the difference between a draw block and a pass block. The draw is usually a quick set. You have to coach against the draw on the pass rush. The second thing you have to know in the I set is this: It is not a pass unless the quarterback has gone as deep as the deepest back. Against the split backs it is easy. It is clear and defined.

If we read the set back and the tackle moves out to pass protect, we want to get into a pass rush. This is our *tilt rush*. All we are trying to do is to be in a position to contain rush after the tackle and guard set to pass block. We want to get our outside hand on the cuff of his shoulder and the inside hand on his pec and stay outside. He must stay outside and keep the containment. He wants to work up the field in a contain position. The most underused rush is the power pass rush. There are two things that come out of this rush. Once you get him in that position, you want to take him straight back.

There is a difference in the pass rush on a back and on a tackle. I do not like to use a flipper on a back. Every now and then, you may need to do that, particularly early in the game, to give them something to think about. I believe in giving them the same thing back. If the fullback comes and cuts your legs out from under you, then I say you can come back and do the same thing to the fullback. On a back, there is a lot of time and a lot of space to make you move. This is where the football players mentally agree to make contact. This is where the good players trick the backs. You must look him right in the eyes, read his shoulder pads, and then do whatever it takes to beat him.

There is another pass rush that we get out of stunting. This is what we want on stunts in our pass rush. We want to get off on the ball, which is your key. You use the proper footwork. First, I will let the players rush their own way. If they do not get the job done, then I tell them to do it my way. I do not have a problem with this. I would prefer a lateral crossover dip, rip, and the whole ball of wax up the field. If a player can get it done his way, that is fine with me.

I believe you have to give the players clues or keys to help them. Let's look at the pass rush versus boot or counter plays. If the tackle sets and turns his rear end to the sideline, we are thinking counter or boot action. Most players want to run upfield when they see the tackle turn his tail. We do not want them to run upfield when they see this. We want them to close down and get their shoulder square to the line of scrimmage. We want to square the pads. We want the head in front of the man.

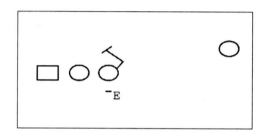

After we get our pads square, and then see it is turnout protection, we step out to keep from getting cut off. We call this containment "Oh crap!" You think you have the play contained, and then you see that it is going outside. That is when you yell out, "Oh crap," and take off to contain. We tell them to run straight to the boundary. We do not want them to go upfield and try to pull up. We want to see through the tackle to the next back or to the next lineman.

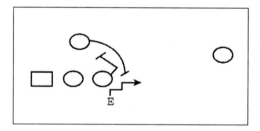

At some point, everyone that plays football must learn to play the cut block. When the tackle steps out, the back comes to cut the end. That is where we must play the cut block. Someone is always throwing at your legs on defense. I am still talking about containment and pass rush. The back is trying to cut the legs of the end. I learned some important things about the cut block that I feel we need to look at a little closer.

The first thing about the cut block is this: When you see the cut block, you had better look at the helmet of the blocker real close. We want to look at that helmet from a bent knee and bent ankle position. Everything in football, I believe, starts and finishes from the bent-knee position. When we see the cut block coming, the man will cut us if we go upfield. We tell them to stay on their feet and we will have a chance. We want to work the line of scrimmage with the shoulders square in a bent-knee position. We want to look at the helmet as we work outside. We do not want the hands on the blocker's back. We want to put both hands on the helmet and press it away and push it all the way to the ground. We want to come out of the block and keep our feet and shoulders square. We do not want to cross over. We play the helmet to the ground and continue on our "oh crap" angle.

I had the privilege, the last two summers, to work in the NFL on a minority program. I worked with Chuck Noll and the Pittsburgh Steelers. I got this term from Chuck. I think all head coaches have one or two terms that they want to tag as special to them. One of his big favorites is this: "Use *same foot, same shoulder.*" If you take a blocker on, you need to take him on with the same shoulder and the same foot. That is your strength and power. Take him on with the shoulder over the knees. This is where the cut block comes into play. *Same foot, same shoulder.* Shoulder over the knees.

I do not tell the frosh the same thing I tell the upperclassmen. As the saying goes at the American Express company, "Membership has its privileges." When you get to be an older player, you can experiment to find out what they can do best. When they are young, we do not want to give them too much. We tell the freshmen to get as wide as they can and still be in a position to take care of their responsibility.

If I am the strike end playing against the 9 technique that is trying to make a reach block on me, this is how I play him. I am looking at the helmet of the end. If his helmet goes inside, I step inside with him. It is a mirror step. We always step with the foot in the direction we are going. I want to smash and attack the outside ear hole of the helmet. I take the outside hand on his shoulder and inside hand and rip through the pec. It ends up on the throat. Now I want to push and pull and work him up the field. Jam that pad up in his throat. Take him up the field, cut off the running lane, and make the play. One problem is when the players start rising up, looking for the ball. When I coached with Tom Harper at North Carolina, he called that "looking over the fence." We contain rush against the sprint-out attack. We can take the fullback on and fight him one on one or we can try to trick him and step outside. You agree to make contact and then you fool him and step outside and contain.

Against the wide splits, we want to make sure we can cover our area. If the end is split up to three yards, he can split the difference. If he is split four yards, we can turn our back to the man and he cannot clip us. Anytime we are on a vacated area, or on air, we make it look like we are going to rush. Another thing I learned from Tom Harper was this: I do not spend a lot of time coaching stance. If you spend a lot of time coaching stance, they will never get out of their stance. I do not really care if the man is in a two-point or three-point stance.

On a down block, the end looks at the helmet of the tackle as he comes inside. He is looking at the helmet and he is going to throw his butt inside and squeeze the play down. As he squeezes the play down, he looks off the tail of the tackle to his next key. It could be the near back, guard, or the quarterback. If the near back is attacking him, he wants to play on the line of scrimmage and stay underneath the blocker. If he will stay on the line of scrimmage and close and shuffle, shuffle, and shuffle, he will know where the ball is. After he takes three steps, if nothing is happening, there is a good chance that two things are going on. First, it is going to be a reverse, or second, the play is going away from him.

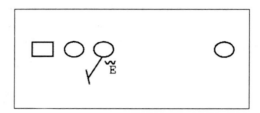

Against the pulling guard, it is the same thing. We still play on the line of scrimmage and stay underneath and hold on as he reads his keys.

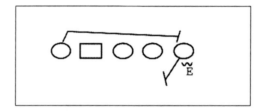

Coach Larry New did not go over our trigger terms. Every position has its own trigger terms. Some trigger terms will overlap. For every angle there is for the end, we have a name for it. If we want him to come underneath the blocker, we call it a *Charlie*. If we want him to go off his butt, we call it a *mesh*. If we want him to go straight up the field, we call it sooie or smash. If we want him to do the same thing, but line up over the head of the tight end, we call it *slit*. That means he steps with the inside foot, and then gets up the field. If we want to run a combination stunt with another man, we give it a name. Everyone has his own terms. I can teach you this system in five minutes. Coach Glaser will cover the base alignments of our front in his lecture.

I do think the end and strike positions can determine the outcome of a game. They can dominate a game just by moving around. I feel good about the people we have coming back to play those two positions for us next year.

The question is asked, "How do we play against two tight ends?" If the offense has two ends and we do not give the end a trigger term, he must look down inside to the nose man. If the nose is lined up on the center gap, he stays on the tackle. If the nose is out on the guard, the end moves outside on the end. I can coach the same thing to both players on this defense. It depends on the experience of the players. If we call a stack, the tackle stays on the tackle and we bring in the rover to play on the tight end. We would treat a slot the same as a tight end.

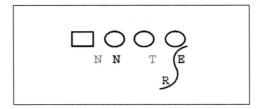

If you want to visit with us, you are welcome. Most of this material we have on tape and you are welcome to see those tapes. I have enjoyed this experience and I hope I have given you something that will help you next year. Thank you.

5

The Outside Linebacker in the 4-3 Defense

Terry Hoeppner
Miami University (Ohio)
2000

Thank you very much. It is truly an honor and privilege to be here. It is good to be back and be with people who understand what I do. After getting off the road from recruiting, I feel like a traveling salesman. Trying to sell your program and school to these recruits is a big job.

When you speak at a clinic, you want to come up with a topic that is applicable to a lot of people. We are a 4-3 defense and have been one for a long time. I can get tape out from 1992-93 and it would be almost what we do right now. We have not changed it very much.

I decided to talk about our outside linebacker play. If you bring anyone off the edge, in any form of defense, this talk is going to help you. That has been the key to our defense. A lot of people use our defense or some version of it. We have great success with the defense. But the key has been our outside linebacker play—we feature that guy. We have had the defensive player of the year in our conference six of the last nine years, and three in a row. Two years ago, they picked two outside linebackers for All-League, and we had them both.

We recruit that type of player. We try to get the guys who have the tools we want them to have to play that position. It is not only because they are great athletes that they are successful—part of it has to be the plan they are put into. I tell our outside linebackers not to get too excited about themselves. We are giving them the opportunity to become great players. We are looking for guys that can run, are tough, but have good qualities. These guys are smart football players. I tell them I can get them aligned right and teach them the proper techniques, but, when it comes to playing, they have to use the instincts they have. They've got to make plays.

Woody Hayes talked about the O.J. Simpson run in his book *Hotline to Victory*. He said there was the action, the reaction, and the re-reaction. That is what the special players have. We look for the same type of guys. They are football players that can go beyond on their instincts. The most important thing to those guys is making the play.

Today, I'm going to talk about what we do with our outside linebackers. I'm going to be pretty specific about it and concentrate on the split-side linebacker. That is where people try to attack us away from the tight end.

Our basic defense has changed, and it starts with a plan. Everybody has a plan. I spent some time in Alabama when I was getting to play a little football. If any of you get fired, go down to Jefferson County, Alabama, in the winter and get a job. That is when they hire their coaches. I got a coaching job in the off-season. You can walk in any mall in Birmingham and see the Alabama store. On the other side of the mall is the Auburn store. If you go into the Alabama store, you will find a plaque about Bear Bryant's sayings. On one is the saying: "Have a plan, work the plan, and plan for the unexpected." We have a plan on defense. Our success as a defense will be determined by how well we accomplish our goals. To be the best defense in the Mid-American Conference we must:

- Stop the run consistently.

- Be great in the red zone.

- Eliminate SIW's—that means self-inflected wounds. We led the league in penalties last year.

- Be an intimidating defense—both in our style of play by being physical and in our tactics by being multiple.

- Be a smart defense. Know the game situation and what our opponent is likely to do in that situation.

- Play with emotion and trust. Care greatly about the outcome and your performance, and have faith in your teammates and coaches.

People try to spread us out. Therefore, we would like people to get into two backs a couple of times per series. If people play two backs against us, we will have something for you. We'll gang the line of scrimmage and get a lot of people there. We are not an eight-man front. Everyone says you have to get the eighth man into the box. We are a nine-man front. We have very aggressive safeties and outside linebackers.

Our goal is to give up only 16 points or less per game. We arrived at that number from some studies we have done. If we do that, we will be in the top 10 in scoring defense. Plus, we will be in every game we play. In modern-day college football, that is hard to do.

One of the greatest compliments I've ever received came from an official. He turned to me on the sideline and said, "I've got to keep counting. It seems like you've got more guys out there than you are supposed to." We didn't, but I liked the thought.

There is a challenge in today's football for a guy to take personal responsibility for the outcome of the game—it is important to him. This is having pride in what they do on the field.

Let me show you how we line up real quickly. I don't want this to turn into a lecture on 4-3 defense. Our defensive end to the tight end is in a 7 technique. We don't play much 9 technique with the defensive end. Our tackles are in a 3 and weakside 0 shade techniques. The other end is in a 5 technique on the openside tackle. Our base coverage is cover 4. That is a quarter coverage. Most of our defenses are tight end oriented. The Mike linebacker finds the tight end and makes a Roger or Larry call; that obviously means left or right. The one thing I like about this is that we can give you a lot of fronts, but we don't have great adjustments. Even if our opponents know what we do, it doesn't help them that much. You have to know what we are doing in that particular situation. We are going to show you one thing and give you something else. Our defense doesn't have to adjust to anyone much anymore. We dictate to the offense.

The key for our outside linebacker is what we call a "Cat." People like to run at the bubbles in your defense. They like to attack the weakside B gap, strongside A gap, and strongside C gap. Our defense crowds the line of scrimmage and comes as hard as we can. When we send one guy off the edge, that is not a blitz to us. When we bring the outside linebacker off the edge, the end slants into the B gap, and that is not a blitz. We don't have to play man-to-man behind that little stunt.

Part of the advantage is our cover 4. It all starts with our quarter coverage. In reality, the coverage is a 5-under and 2-deep coverage. This coverage allows us to be aggressive with our outside linebackers. The corners basically become the deep-half defenders. The safeties become the robbers in the curl areas. Our outside linebackers are basically responsible for the flats. Our linebackers don't drop. When I first started coaching defense, I was really frustrated by that. I went back to my college coach and asked him, "If I have two guys in my zone, who do I cover?" He told me to cover the one they were going to throw to.

We play a match-up type of coverage. We don't drop our linebackers; we operate in a five-yard line. If you run sprint draw at our linebacker, we step up. Someone else

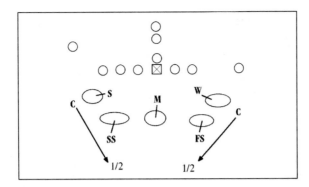

will worry about covering the curls and digs in the hole. As a linebacker, I don't have to get back in coverage. That makes it tough to run screens and draws on us. People don't throw screens on us. We don't drop with our linebackers, so we don't have to react back up—we are already there. Our quarter coverage allows us to get nine guys into the box. If we send the outside linebacker on a Cat, the free safety has to move over and take number 2 weak.

Let me show you our entire defense in our base set, so you can see it and know what I have been talking about.

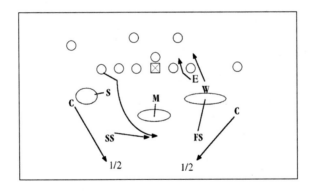

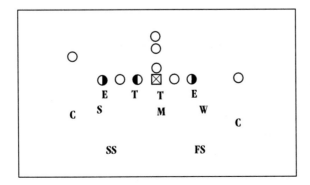

In 1994, when I took over at Miami as defensive coordinator, our leading tackler in the league was our free safety. If your free safety is your leading tackler, the defense must not be very good. We were first in the nation in pass defense and third in total defense. He was defensive player of the year. At free safety, he ran by the linebackers who had to fight off blocks and made the tackle.

Here's what Will Cat does for us. I'll give you an overview first and then get into specifics. We spend a disproportionate amount of time in practice preparing the outside linebacker to do what they have to do. We are going to ask him to come off the edge and do a bunch of things. An example would be the 5 technique coming under into the B gap and Will coming off the edge. One of the Cat's rules is: don't let anyone cross your face. If a back flares and the Will linebacker continues to the quarterback, something bad is going to happen. The quarterback will throw over the Cat's head to the flaring back, who with one block can run forever. In cover 4, Will has to cover the number 2 receiver in the flat. The safety is taking number 2 vertical, and the corners have bailed out to the deep responsibility. That gives you an idea of what we ask him to do.

What I want to do now is go through all the things we ask our outside linebackers to do on the run. As the head coach, I don't have a position to coach. I really miss that, but they do let me run the Cat drill. That is the drill he will be able to do in his sleep. We can call Will Cat or Sam Cat, and bring one, or double Cat and bring them both. We have to adjust the coverage when we do that. We have to play man coverage when we bring both outside linebackers.

What does he see? They key the single back or tailback as they come. They have to know what he is doing. The first thing we do is to bring both backs toward the Will linebacker. He sees the tailback and the fullback running downhill at him. The play is a power slant at the Will linebacker. They are blocking down and kicking out the Will linebacker. The Will linebacker is responsible for containment. But "contain" is a word we don't use in our defense anymore. He has to make this play bounce to the sideline. An ideal running play for us is a play that goes to the sideline. We want to make the tackle for no gain at the sideline. We bounce the play outside and use our speed to run it down.

The Will linebacker wants to get inside the block of the fullback any way he can. We don't want him to sacrifice himself completely. We want him to be a player after the play bounces. But if he has to, he gives himself up and takes the fullback down so that the tailback bounces outside. On the inside, the defensive end is taking the B gap inside. Hopefully, he is protecting our Mike linebacker, who is five yards off the ball inside and keying on the tailback. He comes under and, as the ball bounces outside, he scrapes and makes the play. What I want the Will to do is get inside the block, pry up, and make the play. That is Saturday morning clinic talk—it is hard to do, but it is not impossible.

If the Will linebacker gets kicked out, the integrity of the defense is lost. The Mike linebacker is expecting the ball to bounce, and it is running inside him. That is half the drill. The other half is coming from the other side. This is one of my pet peeves. During the course of a year, you see things that confirm and reconfirm some of your ideas. This is definitely one of them. We have been hurt on a play just like this. The backside Sam linebacker is coming and the tailback is going away. If he continues to sprint upfield, he has a chance to make a play on the bootleg. It is a 1-in-10 chance. If the linebacker runs upfield, he may as well go take a knee.

The Sam linebacker comes across the line of scrimmage and the play is going away from him. There are only a few things that can happen. We try to teach in a series of three. I'm not sure they can handle more than three things. The first thing he has to do is find the football—don't continue running upfield. Only two things can happen: The tailback will cut the ball back or the quarterback will bootleg the ball.

If the quarterback takes the ball, puts it on his hip, and gets outside the Sam linebacker, he had better wish he were born a girl. When I talk about these linebackers coming off the ball, they are not running as fast as they can to get to the spot. We are effective rushers. We make plays. When the opponent sees this coming, they have second thoughts about running the bootleg. They don't want that negative play or the quarterback getting hit right in the mouth.

That is the first part of this drill. It could be run either way, because there is no tight end involved. We want our linebackers to see how tough the fullbacks are. How many tough fullbacks do you really play against? How many of those guys really want to do that kick-out block? They are mad because they don't get to play tailback. How many times are they willing to rock the linebacker? I tell our guys to rock them. When it comes to linemen, it is no way. We don't fight with linemen; they are too big. With the fullback, we want to know who is going to win the battle—we challenge them. Who is going to win the war? It is going to happen sometime during the game. It might happen the first play of the game, so they have to be ready.

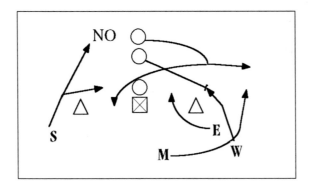

The second thing we work on in the Cat drill is the option. I tell my quarterback, "Bag pitch." He runs the dive play, pulls the ball, and runs option at them. The Will linebacker comes off the edge. We don't want him running up to the pitch man and creating this monster hole for the quarterback to run through. The linebacker has to put on the breaks. He stays on the line of scrimmage, works away, makes the quarterback pitch, and then he turns and makes the play. The trick is not to let the tailback get leverage on him. He is looking at the quarterback, but he has to be aware of the tailback, particularly if the quarterback pitches the ball quickly. We don't want to be chasing the tailback from the inside.

The backside is coming. He finds the football. Everything is going away. The quarterback, tailback, and fullback are going away. If the quarterback fakes or slows down, he can catch the quarterback from the backside. He is set up for the reverse, but I don't ask him to be responsible for that. I don't ask the backside Cat to check reverse.

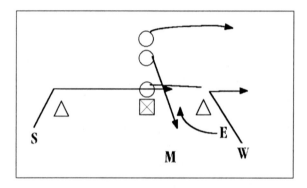

The next thing we do is dropback pass with a flare by the tailback. The rule our linebacker has is: nothing crosses his face. The Cat reads the dropback pass and the back flare. If it is double Cat, someone has him man-to-man. We are not going to take a chance. If that back sees the linebacker coming and releases anyway, something is up. They intend to get the ball to the flare. We come off on the flare across our face. The other side continues his pass rush. We get more sacks from our Cats than anyone else. They are athletic, agile, and aggressive.

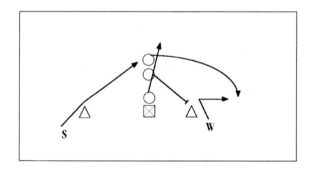

The big theme in spring ball for us is "complete." We lost three great players. We had two in the Senior Bowl and two in the East-West Shrine Hula Bowl. We have a bunch of young, hungry guys, I hope. One of our completion blocking drills will be backs blocking outside linebackers. John Wooden never used the word "win" and didn't talk about winning. He said to play at your best, and winning takes care of itself. I have his book on my desk and there are some things I steal from his book, but I'm into winning and not winning! Who knows what Coach Wooden said behind closed doors?

I believe you have to challenge guys to put it on the line to see what you've got. That's what spring ball to us is all about. We want to find out who the winners are and who the losers are. Everything we do has taken on that aspect. Maybe it affects their psyche. I don't have time for guys with bad psyche when we are losing. We'll council them when they are down, but guess what? Somebody is going to win and somebody is going to lose, and it ain't OK!

In our spring drills, we can have 11-on-11 on just three days. Well, we take a 7-on-7 drill and make it live. This is completion. It is offense versus defense. We use good judgment with the drill, but it is live. We are not trying to get someone killed, but we want the completion. You find out a lot about your receivers in the spring.

We have a change-up to the Cat. Of course, it is called "Dog." That brings the end outside, and the outside linebackers into the B and C gaps. That is good and I like our ends, but it puts them outside doing things I want the outside linebackers doing. We ask the end in the Dog stunt to cover tailbacks if they flare. We do so much Cat; when the Dog does come, it is usually pretty good.

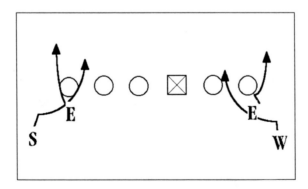

One of our favorite things to do is show the Cat and drop him into coverage. Remember, he has no drop area. When the number 2 receiver comes to the flat, he jumps him and takes him away. If the second receiver goes vertical, the linebacker plays through him to number 1. We don't play curl to flat. We want to cover a man, not ground. If it is a one-back set and the back comes toward the linebacker, he plays normal. If the back goes away, he squeezes the number 2 receiver and allows him no inside releases.

We have variations to our coverage, but if they learn those three things they can play the pass coverage. If the linebacker is showing Cat and the tight end takes off to the flat, the linebacker jumps him in coverage.

The Mike linebacker has a simple pass rule. He has to find the number 3 receiver. He opens to number 3 and defends the tackle box. He doesn't drop. He covers the first receiver into the hook area. In the one-back set, he keys the back and opens to the side the back goes.

We took our fullback, and moved him to Mike linebacker. We had linebackers dropping like flies. In one week he started a game for us at Mike linebacker. Here is what we told him and how we coached him. We told him to play inside-out on the ball. That is all we told him. We let him play instinctively. In pass coverage, we told him to open to the side of the back and cover the guy they were going to throw it to. That was great coaching. The next week he played both ways. He played fullback and middle linebacker. I gave him the game ball. He had eight knockdown passes and a catch for 24 yards. He had seven tackles and the biggest hit we've had from a Mike linebacker in a long time. As of right now, Nick is a Mike linebacker.

With our Cat, we also get into an Eagle defense. This originated as a check for us and became a call. We call Eagle and stem to it. The 3 technique tackle stems to a 5 technique. The shade tackle changes his shade to the strongside. The backside end stems into the B gap. Because we are a 4-3 team, when our end stems into that gap we call that the "ninja technique." When he stems to that gap, the offensive lineman can't see him—he disappears. All he does is run into the backfield and make plays. The Will linebacker comes onto the line of scrimmage and is in his Cat technique. The Sam linebacker moves inside with the Mike linebacker. The only other thing we have to do is make the free safety aware that he has the number 2 receiver weak because the Will linebacker is going.

The other way we can get into the Eagle is by what we call "slant." Our alignments are 5, 3, 0 shade, and 5 technique. The defensive end to the tight end stems to a 7

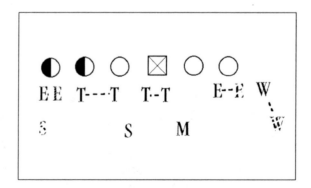

technique. On the snap of the ball, he loops to a 9 technique. That gives the tight end one more thing to think about. The 3 technique tackle slants into a 4i position back up through the back of the offensive tackle. The shade 0 uses a dash or cross-face technique to get on the other side of the center. The 5 technique on the backside uses a gap technique to get inside into the B gap. The Will linebacker runs his Cat on the backside. We have the same defense as the Eagle, but we get it from slanting into it.

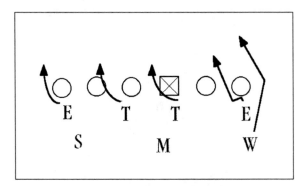

The technique played by the 7 technique end is good against a tight end run. When he loops outside, the Sam linebacker hangs back, doesn't get blocked, and plays the C gap.

The last thing we can do pretty easily is get into the Bear defense. We don't call it that, but that is what it is. We slide the backside end down into a B gap technique. We bring in additional defensive backs or linebackers and play. The Sam and Will linebackers move up and Cat.

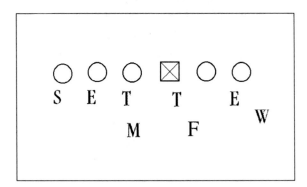

Gentlemen, let's watch this tape of the things I've been talking about. If we can ever do anything for you at Miami, don't hesitate to call. Thank you very much. I hope you guys enjoy the rest of the day.

6

Tennessee Basic Linebacker Drills

Larry Lacewell
University of Tennessee
1991

Men, tonight I am going to talk to you about some things that we have been using for many years on defense. I do not think I am going to offer you any revelations. I think the things that I am going to stress today are the things that have been successful over the years. They are the basic things that we believe in.

We are basically a 4-3 defensive football team. We are a three-linebacker defense. We used to do a lot of things from this defense, but we have quit that. We get them back in their stance in a good football position and let them react to the ball and then play football. I want to cover some of the basic drills that we use to teach our defense.

Warm-Up – Footwork

Purpose: To teach, develop, and maintain quick feet.

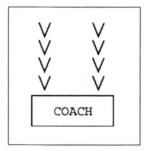

High Knee – Good warm-up drill. I guess it looks impressive, but I don't see many linebackers running like this.

Carioca – I think this is a more realistic drill. We are in a good football position, and we slide the feet, cross over, etc. We are going to get in that bent-knee position, trying to keep our weight forward, and emphasize head up and back straight. We go back and forth, facing each other.

Shuffle – Shuffle back and forth, bent knee, shoulder pads over our knees.

Backpedal – Shoulder pads over our knees and toes.

Reaction – Coach is out in front with a football. He moves the players in different directions, keeping the shoulders square to the goalpost. This is a realistic drill on defense because we have to react to play defense. On defense, we don't get in a huddle and call a play and say, "Let's all run to our right and knock the hell out of the ballcarrier." We have to go into our defensive huddle, call the defense, and then hope that one of us ends up where the ball is. We have to react to that.

Quarter Eagle – I am not really sold on this drill. When I first saw it at the University of Alabama, I thought it was the greatest drill I had ever seen. There might have been something to the first drill, where the coach would say, "Hit, hit," and on the sound the players would do a quarter eagle (half turn, right or left). Then we extended it. We started hitting our hats, then our thighs, etc. In a football game, you never see a player yell out, "Hit, hit," and then hit his helmet, etc.

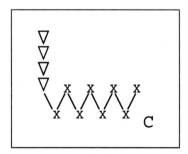

W Drill

Purpose: To work on change of direction. To take wasted motion out of football. *Note*: To add more skill development to the drill, add open field tackling.

We set up cones and the player must sprint to the cones. We are going to sprint to the cone, plant, drop, and go to the next cone. It is just like a linebacker going back on pass defense. He must plant, and then sprint to the next cone, drop and sprint, etc.

Take-On Drill

Purpose: To teach proper mechanics of delivering a blow with the hands. To teach proper stance. To develop and improve the defensive player's ability to hit an explosive lick without losing body control.

We are going to try to deliver a blow with the hands. I used to be a big "forearm flipper" coach. Now, the offensive man blocks with his hands and they will lock up on the flipper. We emphasize hands. It toughens the hands. The sled is braced up against a wall. We teach them to come out of their hips and knees. We start on the ground in a six-point stance. We are really going to extend and explode into the sled. Then we do it from the up position.

We will hit, hit, hit, and after the third hit, they will shuffle out of there. This is the way we want our linebackers to take on the blocker, exploding into him.

Bag Drills

Purpose: To develop foot quickness and body control. To incorporate quick feet and body control with take-on drill. *Note:* To add more development to the drill, add a fumble recovery or angle tackle. Lay the dummies on the ground about two feet apart.

I really think this is football. It simulates running over traffic and running through traffic.

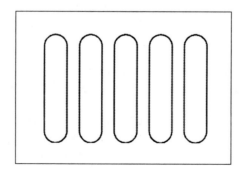

High Knee – We go straight ahead and run over the dummies.

Two Feet in the Hole – We go over the dummy and put both feet on the ground, then go over the next dummy.

Shuffle – We shuffle over each dummy.

Medicine Ball – We take a big old medicine ball and stand the coach or a manager right in the center space between all of the dummies. They try to knock the feet out from under the players. We fire that medicine ball below his knees as fast as we can. This is like a blocker firing out at the defensive man. The defensive man has to drop his body and fend off the blocker (medicine ball) with his hands. Note: We use the medicine ball on our "string out" drill. We throw the medicine ball at the knees of the defensive man, and emphasize the defensive man taking on the blocker (medicine ball). We emphasize "feeling" the football, while keeping your eyes on the inside shoulder of the blocker.

Stance and Step

This is a really simple drill, but we do it every day. We take a coach and put him over on the other side of the dummies that are lying on the ground. Our three linebackers assume their positions. The coach takes the ball and makes a move by taking a step. When he steps, the linebackers step. They get into their stance and they step. We are keying our basic backfield key. We will do what we call a *rock and roll*. It is our misdirection key. The coach will step one way and then step back the other way. The linebackers do the same steps. We do this every day for about five minutes. All we are trying to do is to get them into a good stance and step with the proper foot and not cross over.

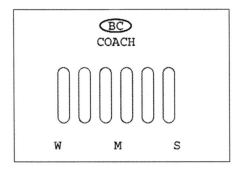

Key Drill with a Ballcarrier

This is the same drill as *stance and step*. Now we put a ballcarrier where the coach was before. The linebackers are all going to their gaps. We have it drawn up here where the ballcarrier would attack. We have what we call *midpoint* and *outside point*. Our linebackers know that they must fill certain gaps. Our linebackers are five yards deep.

I know that is awfully deep. We stress downhill moves. We do not move laterally as much as move downhill. Our linebackers know, "If that ballcarrier moves to my point, the first thing I am going to do is to go downhill. I am not moving laterally." (If we see the toss sweep, we will move laterally.) When we are five yards deep, we have more of an angle, and the blockers have a hard time getting to us. (I have the option of moving the linebackers closer if need be.)

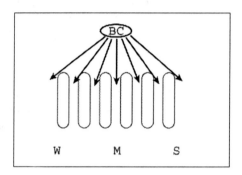

Key Drill/Blocking Scheme

Now we are going to take the big picture. We are going to put the linemen up there. We have basic keys. I am not trying to tell you what defense to use. You use your own defense. We try to see through the linemen in front of us to the near back. We do not really want to see the quarterback. It amazes me how the quarterback will reverse out, and we will step that way, when we are not even keying him.

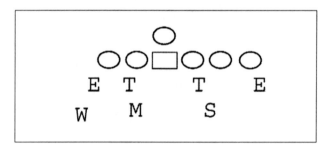

This is not a full-contact drill. So, we use anyone that is available—managers, etc. We key every possible play. We run the outside veer, option, trap, etc. We have the quarterback open up. The linemen are going to block down, and we are going to take our same key steps and slide like we did in our original key drill.

Next, we block the center backside, pull both guards, bring the other linemen down, and we rock and roll. Our Will linebacker will yell out, "Guard, guard, guard." Now our Mike linebacker and our Sam linebacker are alerted that the guards are coming

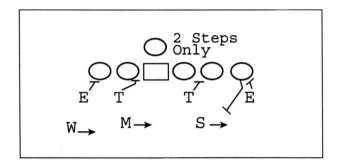

their way. When Mike and Sam hear "guard," they freeze right on the spot. We hope that they will see it too, but if they don't, they have been alerted. We do this every day.

We go a little further with this drill. We get our first-line people in this drill. It is mainly a defensive drill. The offensive people don't like this drill. You can go as tough as you want and we really get this thing going good. You can have a quick whistle if you want. The guard pulls, and the tackle and end block down. Everything starts out just like it is going to be a running play. All we do is blow the whistle after a couple of steps on each play. We just do this same drill over and over and over.

Two Steps Read Drill

We will cut down as much as we can on defense. We are doing more and more of this today. We will have a Sam and a Mike on one side, and on the other side, we have a Mike and Willie working. We do what we call *half-line drills*. We get more out of this than anything else we do. We like to tape this drill from the backside.

We are more interested in repetitions than anything else. The biggest mistake that many coaches make, in terms of drills, is that they want to talk too much. They want to overcoach them on the field. The best thing to do is *repetition, repetition, repetition*.

We will put our Mike linebacker in against a center, two guards, and a backfield. We run various combinations with the center blocking back, with one guard pulling, and the other guard blocking on the Mike linebacker. We look at all the blocking combinations.

Tackling Drills

Form Tackling – We want to make sure the shoulders are warmed up before we start tackling.

Angle Tackling – Ballcarrier runs on an angle. Linebacker will attack on an angle through the point of aim with proper tackling form. We are trying to get our headgear into the ball.

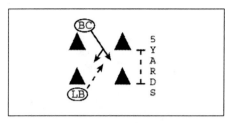

Eye-Opener – Linebacker shuffle keeping backside leverage on the ballcarrier and attacking when the ballcarrier is committed to a hole. Drive through point of aim with proper tackling form, explode, put the headgear on the football, and lock the hands around him. We do not know what hole the ballcarrier is going to hit.

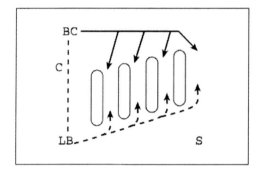

Open Field Tackling – Linebacker closest to the ballcarrier giving the ballcarrier only one direction to go. Attack point of aim and use the proper tackling form.

Coaching Point: Force ball to sideline when possible.

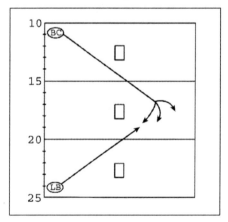

There are different opinions on open field tackling. We have gone through the years, where we sprinted up to the ballcarrier and then broke down a few yards in front of him. There are people today teaching the tackler to stay up. In other words, they tell the tackler to go as hard as he can to the ballcarrier, give him one angle to go, and tackle him high, and keep him on his feet. We are now at the point where we sell out and try not to break down too soon.

7

Linebackers in the 4-3 Scheme

Rick Lantz
University of Virginia
1995

Good afternoon gentlemen. It's nice to be here. I don't know if I can talk about defense after hearing Dan Young of Nebraska talk about all those counter sweeps and traps. I hope the defense can stand up to that type of offense.

Let me start out by saying, football is not revolutionary. It is an evolutionary process. There are no magical defenses or offenses. You simply believe in something and coach it. You constantly try to find better ways to do things. Ten years ago, we began to shift from a 5-2 to a 4-3 defense. However, I still consider myself to be a 5-2 football coach. We are still using 5-2 terminology with our 4-3 defense.

The topic that was given to me today was linebacker techniques. As soon as I hear "linebacker techniques," I think about stance, shed, explosion, and things like that. I'm going to talk about some of those things. However, I'm going to try and make people understand how we teach the defense first. Where we get lined up is not the most important thing in this lecture. I'm more concerned about how the players fit into the defensive scheme. My talk today is going to be based around how we get people to be good football players.

Football is a mental game. Most of what a player does comes from his head. Don't get me wrong, being a great athlete helps tremendously. This past year, I had the chance to coach the fastest defensive team I've ever been associated with. We had two outside linebackers who could run in the 4.5 range. That means their techniques got a little better. They didn't have to be perfect all the time to make the plays. What we are trying to do is get them where they are perfect in their technique all the time. If a player doesn't have a basic understanding of the game, it doesn't make any difference how he looks in a stance. If he doesn't have that understanding, he will be making wrong decisions about 50 percent of the time.

Football is the ultimate team game. You have 11 people on each side of the ball acting and reacting with certain assignments to carry out. When the ball is snapped, everything starts to change. They have to make adjustments on the fly.

In our playbook, we have written a philosophy. The first thing in that philosophy is to have a total understanding of the concepts of team defense. How does the ball carrying threat affect me and the people around me? When we talk about linebacker techniques, we are talking about how we get to the football and make plays.

The game of football is simple. You can line up the defense any place you want. When the ball is coming toward me, my responsibility and reaction is to people outside of me. When the ball is going away from me, my responsibility is based on the presnap read or a reaction to a blocking scheme of people to my inside. Defense is not just being tough, hard, or loving the game of football. It is understanding where the player fits into the total scheme.

We teach this understanding of the game by what we call a "requirement system." We have very specific requirements for every defensive call we make. These things don't change. They have nothing to do with ability at all. The first thing we have to do is get in the proper stance and get aligned correctly with the call. We, as football coaches, are not smart enough to have a universal set of football terms. We have to have our own set of words. People all over the country call the same defense different things. Coach Bob Davie showed you a defense called a stacked 3-5 this morning. We call the same defense a 50 shade. But regardless of the name, the players have to get aligned properly in whatever defense is called. There is no excuse to be out of position. If they are in the wrong position, they do up-downs till they know it. God tells them they have to do that. If they don't, they do penance because I'm a Catholic.

They have to know their presnap gap responsibility. When I call the 50 shade defense, I have a defensive tackle in a 3 technique to the tight end side and defensive tackle in a 5 technique to the split end side. The linebackers have to know their gap responsibility when the ball comes to them or goes away. If I add a stunt that changes his presnap gap, he has to know and understand that. There is no excuse for not knowing that.

They also have to know what their paired key is. We are always looking through the linemen to the backs. We don't think you can key the lineman you aligned on and be right 100 percent of the time. If they key the backs only, the same thing is true. They have to be able to look through the linemen to the backs and know what they do on the snap of the ball. At some point, they get comfortable to the point that even though they can't tell me what the linemen did in front of them, I can tell by their reaction that they knew.

The linebacker has to know the defensive responsibility of the defensive linemen on the outside and inside of him. The defensive lineman has a presnap responsibility and a reaction responsibility. If the offensive lineman blocks him, he plays his gap responsibility. However, if he blocks down, he has a reaction responsibility of dive, trap, cutback, and pursue, in that order. The defensive lineman closes to the inside and plays his reaction responsibility. The linebacker's responsibility changes with that movement. The linebacker's presnap gap was taken by a reaction key of the defensive lineman. Now, the linebacker's gap changes. In addition to the run key, the linebacker has to know his pass responsibility if it is a pass play. He is either zone or man, but he must know.

We spend a lot of time talking about quality. Our product is performance. When Ty Smith, Trent Walters, Bob Maddox, and I were shifting the defense from a 5-2 to a 4-3 at the University of Louisville, we were not a very good football team. After Coach Schnellenberger's first year at Louisville, we were the 106th rated defense in America. I was out of work, so I came to help him. We began to improve, and it wasn't through teaching technique. We started demanding that our kids do the right things. We started to develop this "quality program." We talked about it all the time. We stressed things in practice like running to the ball.

I will never forget the year we first went into the 4-3 defense. We had a practice one day in the spring. Mike Flores, who now plays for the Eagles, was participating in a blitz period. We filmed all our drills. This was a full-speed drill with the best on the best. We didn't hit the quarterback, but everything else was live. Mike would sprint up the field after the quarterback. After the ball was thrown, he would turn and sprint downfield to the ball. He was working his butt off. He did it play after play. We were not going to practice the next day, but the kids were going to come in and watch tape. After looking at the tape of Mike, I told Ty Smith that if anyone came over to watch the tape, to show them the tape of Mike in the blitz drill. I wanted the team to see the way he practiced because that is the way I wanted them to go at things.

The next day we got a piece of posterboard and titled it "Quality Club." We put Mike's name on the board with a black magic marker. When the kids wanted to know what Mike's name was doing on the board marked "Quality Club," we told them it was because he knows how to practice. If he doesn't practice the way he is supposed to, we cross his name off the list. A couple days later we put up another name. We started to build on this club. The quality system was a conforming of the requirement of their position. This system didn't take a lot of ability to conform to, but it took a lot of guts and courage.

We want to prevent the errors before they occur. Our rule for defensive linemen is to get as close to the ball as they can. Take all the referee will allow. The price you pay on defense is greater than the offense. On defense, we don't have the luxury of the punt. A guy lining up offside could hurt the defense badly. The first time I heard the statement that the defense can't punt was right here at this clinic. A guy by the name of Gary Darnell, who was at Notre Dame at the time, made that statement, but I adopted it as my own.

We had a freshman who played for us this year. He had 200 snaps and was offside nine times. The three things we wanted the defense to understand in our quality system was: one, you can't punt on defense; two, you don't run half a football game; and three, our job is to outplay the opponent's defense. We are trying to keep them from making a mistake in doing things they can control. The standard of performance is "do it right the first time—do it right every time." We are looking for zero defects. We measure our conforming to the requirements by the price you pay for not conforming.

Some people believe you are either a slant team or a straight-ahead team. Because the defense is changing, you can't teach it both ways. They don't want their linebackers having to change gap responsibilities. We are going to teach 50 shade and the counterpart 40 shade with penetration so that the linebacker's gap responsibility is going to change with the reaction of the defensive line or a stunt we are running. The 50 shade defense is a four-man front with the line shifted toward the tight end.

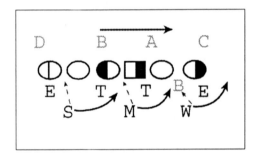
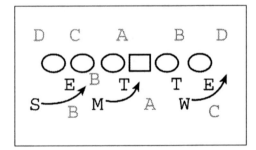

The 40 shade is the same alignment except the line is shifted to the split end or openside of the set. The linebackers in both defenses shift the opposite of the line.

Last year, we ran 759 total offensive plays against our defense. That was either run or pass. What we counted were official plays, where the quarterback received a snap. In 436 of those plays, we were doing something other than playing straight. That meant for every one time these guys played straight, there was 1.7 times when something else was happening. Eighty-three times we put all four down linemen into a predetermined pass rush charge. We did that more than any other single call. That was easy for the linebackers because it gave them a gap to cover, regardless of anything else. However, more times than not, somebody was running a stunt where the linebackers would be affected by the charge of the line. I am only bringing that up because of this. All the penetration and cross charges sometimes came about as an automatic call. If the defensive line was playing straight football and a pass developed, they would automatically go into a cross charge pass rush.

We teach straight charges on Tuesday and all penetrating charges on Wednesday, as a rule. This allows our players a chance to become proficient in their techniques. We are constantly working on things that will help the linebackers with their reaction responsibility. We feel like they can play the presnap read fine. When we teach our pass rush charges in the spring, we never run them against a pass to start with. We always play them against the run. That gives them a chance to understand how to play the defense. When I say "running plays," I'm not talking about draw plays. We are actually running offensive game plan run plays.

I want to go to some underneath pass coverage for the linebackers and how we teach the coverage. The biggest change I see from high school to college is playing pass defense for the linebackers. When I scout kids at linebacker, I don't think too much about their pass coverage, because I don't know what they are being taught. Most of them are taught to go to a certain spot, get parallel to the line of scrimmage, and play the football. Sometimes the quarterback throws them the ball. We are a zone pass defense team. That is what we believe in. We play about 90 percent of the snaps with four down linemen, three linebackers, and four defensive backs in the game. We have coached the nickel scheme; but it seems every time I start to coach that, we get defensive backs hurt. I don't know whether there is a correlation between those two things or not.

It is important for our linebackers to know whether we are in a five-, four-, or three-underneath scheme. If we are playing a four-man rush/two-deep scheme, we have five underneath zones to cover. In that scheme, four of the five people have only one zone to cover. We have one person running a hook to curl scheme. If we have a four-rush/three-deep scheme, then the four underneath people are going to have a multiple zone responsibility. Our basic goal is to make the offense throw the ball outside to the widest receiver. The four underneath defenders are covering curl to flat in the outside zones and hook to curl on the inside zones. All of them have a duel zone responsibility, depending on the initial threat.

We talk about these things in linebacker pass coverage. One of the requirements for the linebacker is to know his pass coverage responsibility. His alignment is going to be dictated by the formation. We start off teaching the regular pro formation with two backs in the backfield. From there, we go to the one-back set, and so on. If we are playing our primary cover, which is a two-deep zone coverage called "blue," the strong outside linebacker has the hook to curl zone to his side.

If I were teaching this in high school, I would choose a shallower aiming point than the college drop. I would teach a 10-yard aiming point rather than the 12 yards for the college game. The high school game is a shorter game for the linebackers. Their aiming point is a spot 10 yards deep and two yards outside of the tight end. When the linebacker reads pass, he should open his hips to the spot but not do anything for an instant. He keeps his head inside for an instant, and then proceeds to his 2-by-10 aiming point. The Mike linebacker is going to open on the exact same angle and go to a spot 10 yards deep and two yards inside the tight end. We don't want to be in a big hurry to get out because we have to look for the draw first. Plus, we don't want to beat the tight end up the field. The draw comes quickly, and we don't want to retreat so fast that the tight end stops at six yards to catch the ball. We want to wall the tight end off, not beat him to the spot. The right linebacker is going to get his shoulders open to his outside and run to a spot 10 yards deep and two yards inside the tight end's alignment.

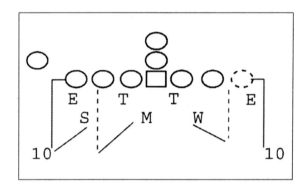

The next thing I want to do is show you how we teach this type of technique. Some of the things we are teaching may be beyond the things you want to teach. But this is what we do. Let me start with the Mike linebacker. His aiming point is 10 yards and two yards inside the tight end. As he starts, the first threat to him is the tight end. The vision of the Mike linebacker goes from checking for the draw, to the tight end to see what he is doing. The problem we have had in the passing game is that our people get too wide before they get depth. That included both the linebackers and the defensive backs. They widen outside of their spot and leave a gap between defenders because we are defending from the inside out. Even our corners make that mistake. They think that because the receiver is making an outside move, they have to rush to a spot outside the receiver. The receiver makes the good inside move and the defenders have created a gap that is too big to cover. The corner has gotten too far away from the next defender who is coming from the inside.

The Mike linebacker opens to the tight end, but he does not get in a hurry. He wants the tight end to beat him upfield because we are playing underneath coverage. If the tight end starts up the field, the Mike linebacker starts on his collision course to wall him off. After he does that and starts to his spot, he gets his vision back on the quarterback. He wants to look to the quarterback to see if the quarterback is going to throw the ball to the tight end. The quarterback will look at the tight end if he is going to throw the ball to him.

The second thing the tight end could do is run a shallow crossing pattern. That means he is vacating the Mike linebacker's area of responsibility. The Mike linebacker is reading through the line into the backfield to his running back key. He reads the running back being handed the ball or setting up to block. As the tight end vacates his area, he must pick up the running back to see if he is coming out on pattern. If the tight end is too shallow, the linebacker doesn't try to stop him. He yells "cross," and throws his arm toward the right linebacker. The reason we throw the arm is for a visual key to the other linebacker. We play in some loud stadiums. The other linebacker may not hear the word "cross," but he may see the motion of the Mike linebacker. Also, by throwing his arms toward the right linebacker, it gets the Mike linebacker's hips opening to his next responsibility. If the Mike linebacker sees the running back widen to the outside, the strong linebacker will start to widen from hook to curl. The Mike linebacker's responsibility now goes from strongside hook to weakside hook. He now plays behind the tight end. The running back is in a no-cover zone. All the Mike linebacker wants to do is tackle the receiver and limit him to what he got on the catch. Anytime the receiver can catch the ball and keep running, we have a problem. If we can't afford to allow the receiver to catch the ball in that situation, then we shouldn't be in a zone coverage.

You can't cover everything, and one of the things we have tried to do is prevent our players from having to play a bunch of different things. We want to play the same coverage in a number of different ways. Don't try to make one coverage do everything. If you want a different reaction by the defense, call a different coverage. If you want them to jump backs coming out of the backfield, call a man coverage.

The last thing that can occur is a combination pattern up the field by the tight end and running back. The Mike linebacker is a hook defender. When he sees this type of situation, he deepens up and gets vision on the quarterback. We are a zone coverage football team so that we can gang up on the thrown ball. In the last four years, we have intercepted 12, 17, 22, and 27 balls. That does not count balls intercepted on two-point tries and things like that. The linebackers have intercepted their share of those balls. However, not one time did a linebacker square himself to the line of scrimmage and intercept a pass.

This year, 13 of the 27 passes intercepted were by linebackers. They intercepted the ball by rolling into the coverage and catching it like a receiver running a pattern. When linebackers square to the line of scrimmage, they can be seen by the quarterback easily. If they will get to their spot, drift and see the quarterback, they can intercept the ball.

The linebacker wants to get into a position to break in the direction the quarterback is attempting to throw the ball. Since 1989, we've had a few Mike linebackers score touchdowns off interceptions. This kid I had this year at Virginia, scored six touchdowns in his career off interceptions. He even intercepted an extra point try and ran it back. That one didn't even count. We think that drifting into the coverage is much better than teaching your kids to get squared up to the line of scrimmage. Don't give the quarterback too much credit—they can't key everybody. They have an initial key, and they throw the ball off that key. We want the quarterback to throw the ball between two linebackers so we can use our reaction to intercept the ball.

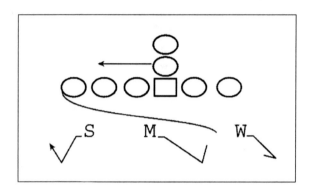

I practice the drift technique every day that I do ball drills. We don't do ball drills every day, but when we do, I use this drill. I stand on the line and make them locate a spot for their drop. They start on their correct angle toward the hash marks when I pat the ball. I make them open their hips toward that spot. If they are not opening toward that spot, I stop them and make them do it again. They keep vision on me, and they are allowed to turn their eyes only once toward their spot. If they have wandered off-line, they have to stop and start over again. When they get close to the spot, I look at them, turn my shoulder in, and throw the ball right down the line that I am on. I expect them to come back on an angle to the ball. I want them to gain ground on the ball. I throw the ball at a good pace. I am not trying to outsmart them; I am trying to make them understand that they can have their shoulders opening to their hook drop and still react to the throw. When they see the shoulders of the quarterback point toward the target, they have to react and break on the thrown ball. I don't let them get to their spot. I want them to react to what I am doing. I pat the ball and they open their hips. I hold the ball up and they start on their track to the spot with their eyes on me. When I turn my shoulder, they come off their drop and react back on an angle to the ball. We do it to both sides and make them break in both directions to make the interception.

I don't want them to come flat or lose ground coming to the ball. If he does that, the receiver will come inside him and make the reception because he will beat the linebacker to the ball. Our goal is to make them throw the ball between any two linebackers on the intermediate passes. You can't do this on a thrown flat pass; but on anything from the curl on in, I want this technique. By using this technique, the teams who run the tight end choice patterns will find the opposite linebacker making the interceptions. The tight end will run his pattern off the strong linebacker and run into the Mike linebacker as he runs his route.

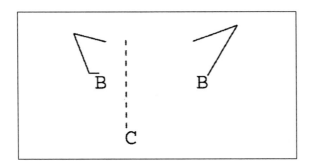

When we have what we call a "zone pass" by the offense, we play it the same. The strong linebacker has the inside curl zone, which is 10 yards and two yards outside the tight end. If the tight end makes an inside stem, the strong linebacker doesn't get any more width. The reason for this is we have two people outside him on the wide receiver or running back going flat. The corner is outside short and the safety is up inside and deep.

If the Mike linebacker can read the numbers of the tight end coming up the field, he fights him up the field and walls him off from the strong hook zone. If the tight end goes underneath and all the Mike linebacker sees is the top of his shoulders, he lets him go. He moves back toward that side to see what is happening. If his weak linebacker is there because his key blocked, the Mike linebacker lets the tight end go. If the weak linebacker is gone, the Mike linebacker has to move his entire zone to cover the tight end. The strong linebacker has vision on the quarterback, so if the tight end tries to work back, he can make the play.

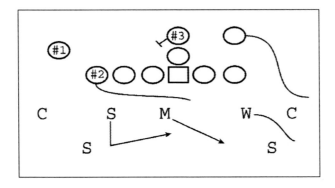

We are a pattern reaction team. We don't run with vertical patterns with our linebackers unless the man that is trying to get deep is the number 3 receiver out of the backfield. If we get an under call from one of the other linebackers, they play their original zones. When the linebackers run deep with the 3 receiver, they are trying to get the quarterback to put some air under the ball. That gives the defensive back time to react to the ball. We do not go from zone to man-to-man in the same defense. We are pattern read in our zones. Pattern read, to our offensive coaches, means that if one man leaves the defender's zone, he runs like hell to pick up the next man in his zone or someone coming into his zone.

If the third receiver comes out of the backfield and runs up the field or threatens the hook zone, we have to make adjustments. The tight end starts to the flat, and the running back comes out and up the field into the hook zone. The strong linebacker sees the tight end go to the flat. He looks inside and sees the running back coming into the hook zone. The running back becomes the strong linebacker's responsibility.

The Mike linebacker's first threat is the tight end, so he sees the end going to flat. The Mike linebacker knows something is coming. He is not man-to-man on the tight end, but he has to feel the pattern. When the tight end starts to the flat and runs the V-cut back to the inside, the Mike linebacker has to have that responsibility. This is a tough pattern because there are two receivers in the Mike linebacker's hook zone. If the running back hooks outside, that is easy for the strong linebacker to cover. But if he hooks inside, like I would run the pattern, the strong linebacker has to fight like hell to get underneath that pattern.

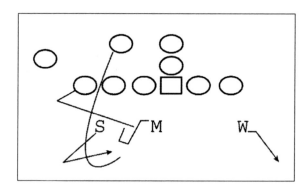

If the offense comes out in a balanced set in the middle of the field, that is tough for us. We won't know where the coverage is going until the number 3 receiver makes his move. The double slot or two tight ends and two flankers is hard to cover. If the ball is on the hash mark, we would predetermine our coverage to the field in a balanced set. The Mike linebacker has to go in the direction of the number 3 receiver—nothing in his technique changes.

If the 3 receiver goes to the defense's left, the Mike linebacker opens left and looks for the tight end to that side. The weakside linebacker opens right and becomes a hook defender. From that point on, the responsibilities of the linebackers are the same. The Mike linebacker is only a hook defender. He has either the strong hook or weak hook, but never a curl zone. The strong and weak linebackers are hook to curl defenders.

If the tight end crosses, the Mike linebacker calls "cross" and becomes the weakside hook defender. The weak linebacker is a weakside hook defender. The first threat to his area is the tight end to his side. If both tight ends are crossing, the linebackers play the same technique. The weak linebacker calls "cross," which switches the Mike linebacker to the strongside hook. What has happened is the Mike and weak linebackers have exchanged zones. The Mike linebacker has the strong hook zone and the weak linebacker has the weak hook zone that could expand into the weakside curl if the tight end continues to run.

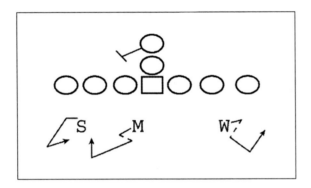

We defend the formation in conjunction with the field. If there is a twin set into the boundary, the Mike linebacker does tip that way. He is going to back up into the field, but he is looking at the receivers into the boundary. We tell our strong linebacker never to get width into the boundary. But the Mike linebacker knows that sometimes the strong linebacker gets expanded out of the hook into the curl area. With the ball on the hash mark, you will see our boundary linebacker back straight up until he sees where the quarterback is looking. As soon as he reads the quarterback's motion, he opens those hips and gets moving. The same is true of the Mike linebacker.

When the linebackers read the tight end trying to get deep, we try to disrupt him. We work our butt off on trying to disrupt patterns. We have knocked the receivers down a bunch of times. There are three phases to pass defense. The first one is to rush the passer so he has to throw the ball before he is ready. The second phase is to cover the receivers or zones so the quarterback can't throw on time. The third is to disrupt the patterns of the receivers so the timing of the quarterback is destroyed. Deep throws are timing throws. It only takes a bump to throw off the timing.

I don't know if any of this stuff made any sense. Playing pass defense is not complicated—playing pass defense is fun. Coaching the secondary is not fun sometimes. It becomes a hell of a lot easier if you get pressure on the quarterback. If we can knock the quarterback down or hit him, it gives us a better chance. It is a game of decision-making and underneath coverage. The problems we had the first two years were: one, they didn't get deep enough first; two, they got too wide too fast; and three, they overplayed the outside. The strong safety who gets beat on the out and up because he was worried about getting too wide too fast. The linebacker who let them complete the pass inside of him because he didn't force the outside throw. Our primary rule is to stay inside the intended receiver and make them throw the ball outside, which is a longer and tougher throw.

Gentlemen, thank you. We would love to see some of you people from Kentucky come to see us. Thanks. I have really enjoyed this.

8

Linebacker Techniques and Drills

Mike Major
University of Kentucky
1998

It is a real honor for me to be here today. The University of Kentucky football staff is honored to be able to speak at this clinic. We hope we can give you some ideas and maybe you can help us out. We really enjoy talking to high school coaches.

The other day I was kind of looking around in the chest of drawers. I found a box in there. I opened it up and there were about eight golf balls and two or three hundred-dollar bills. My wife saw me looking in the box and got really upset at me. She said that box was personal to her. I thought by the way she acted that it was something bad. I thought it couldn't be too bad because all there was in there was about eight golf balls and the money. I asked her what it all meant. She told me that every time we had bad sex, she put a golf ball in that box. We've been married about 12 years, so I was feeling real good. Just eight times in 12 years is not too bad. I asked her what the hundred-dollar bills were? She told me that every time she gets a dozen golf balls, she took them to the pro shop and sold them. It is a matter of attitude.

At the University of Kentucky, we try to do things that are unconventional. A lot of people talk about the way we play football at Kentucky. We try to do things that are very practical. But the game has changed so much over the years. I saw a playoff game in Texas between a school from Houston and a school from Dallas. The Dallas team was ranked high in the nation. The team from Houston was not ranked at all. It was late in the game and the Houston team was ahead by seven points. The Dallas team was driving the ball down the Houston team's throat. There were three minutes left in the game. The Houston coach called time-out, called his kids to the sidelines, and told them to let the Dallas team score on the next play. He told his kids that he wanted the ball the last three minutes of the game. In Texas playoffs back then, there was no overtime rule. The team with the most penetrations is awarded the game if it ends in a tie. He was ahead on penetrations and he believed his offense could drive the ball and win the game. That is what happened and he won the game with a lesser team. He had a great offense but his defense was no better than average.

The light went on in Coach Mumme's head. That was kind of the way things were at the school we were coaching. We didn't have a lot of great athletes, but we had a lot of skill-type kids. If we could come up with an offense that could score a lot of points, we could get away with a lesser defense. We would play a high-risk defense, which would attack and try to create turnovers. We want to play to win, not play to just play. That is the way we play defense.

Hal tends to go for the first down on fourth down. If we get outside the 40-yard line, that is fourth down territory for us. We went for the first down on fourth down 42 times this year. We made 80 percent of them. We didn't play much field position and never have. We gave up a lot of scores. We tend to do that because of the way we play offense. We went from 90th in the nation to somewhere in the 60s on defense. That is a pretty good jump. We had more sacks, interceptions, and turnovers than they have been having here. We got the football back for the offense, which let them set all those records. Basically, that was all we were trying to do. When we go out on defense, we are trying to make the play, not stop the play. We are going to make something happen and beat you at the point of attack. The way to do that is to have quick and fast kids. We take speed over size all the time. We like aggressive kids inside. We are in a run league in the SEC, but to win the championship we have to beat Florida, Tennessee, LSU, Georgia, and Alabama. All those teams are throwing the football. Even Alabama, who has run the ball in its history, is throwing the ball now.

There are four things I look for in a linebacker. I want to know if he is aggressive at the point of attack, if he will butt up in there and knock the ballcarrier back—that is the kind I'm looking for. We must have kids who have C.O.D.—change of direction. We find those types of kids by testing. We run our kids in the 40-yard dash. The next thing we do is called the *pro shuttle*. The pros use this as an indicator also. The kid starts in the middle. He runs five yards and touches a line to his right with both feet. He sprints 10 yards in the other direction and touches the line with both feet the other way. Then he runs five yards back to the middle where he started and is timed. We subtract that time from his 40 time. If the results are between 4.4 or 5.0, you've got a guy who can change direction rapidly. That is the guy who can start, go back, retrace his steps, and still make the play.

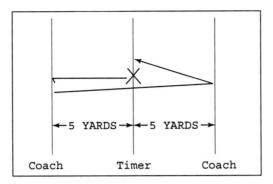

We are a downhill football team. We do everything on the diagonal with our linebacking corps. We line them up with their heels at five yards, and they attack the line of scrimmage on a diagonal path. We are not a shuffle football team.

The next thing we look for is great intelligence. We want a guy who can think while he is out on the football field. A linebacker is a guy who is making adjustments at the point of attack and trying to decide what he needs to do. They cannot be panic-type guys. If one of our guys makes the wrong decision, I can live with it as long as he goes hard. If he stops, I can't live with that.

The last thing we look for in our linebackers is a guy who can cover in the passing game. He understands about pass coverage. There are a lot of guys who can play inside and are great on the running game, but they can't play the pass.

We have some guys at Kentucky who are great blitzing and covering linebackers. There are very few guys who can do that. We try to play situation football all the time. We substitute according to situation. When it gets to the in-between downs, we play the pass.

We are a 4-3 front. We have a Sam, Mike, and Willie linebacker. The personalities of these players are all different. The hardest guy to find is the Mike linebacker. He has to really play with his eyes. He has to have great vision. He has things happening to both sides of him and he can't lose orientation to where he is. We work with the Mike linebacker a lot during the off-season. We tell him to key the backs with the top of his eyes. He sees the two guards and the center through the bottom of his eyes. We never look at the quarterback because he is a lying S.O.B. The quarterback will get you in trouble if you watch him. If you have a Mike linebacker that is false keying, it is because he is looking at the quarterback.

The Sam and Willie linebackers are a little easier to play. The Sam linebacker is a blitzing-type linebacker in our scheme. That is contrary to what they do at Nebraska or Florida State. They do it the other way. We understood that, but we felt if we blitzed from the strongside, the tight end would have to do something. If we can take the tight end out of the passing scheme, that is a release we don't have to worry about. The offense has to play 4 blocker to the strongside, because of the blitz possibility from Sam and Mike. People tend to put the tight end into the field. We blitz from the fieldside and cock the secondary the other way.

The Willie linebacker is more of a run-and-cover type guy. We want the speed linebacker at the Willie position. We want a 4.4 or better playing the Willie linebacker. Our Sam linebacker is 4.5 or better. We can get by with a 4.6 linebacker in the middle, although we want them as fast as we can get them. Size does not matter. However, this year I reversed my thinking a little. I think you need more height in the middle because of the "dig" routes we get. We picked these things up from the Cowboys and the Washington State people. I looked at Washington State. They were last in their conference on defense, but they went to the Rose Bowl. I saw some things they did a little differently with the 4-3. I also watched the Nebraska–Tennessee game in the Orange Bowl. Nebraska did some things with its zone scheme that we are going to try to put in this spring.

The linebackers have to be great students of the game of football. Just being a hitter doesn't make you a great linebacker. Great hitters will tend to get you in a bind more than they will help you. If I've got a great hitter, I'll put him on the defensive line and he can punch all the time. All the linebackers and strong safeties we moved up. We play them at five yards instead of nine yards.

During our training, we don't worry about the bench press. Before we got here, Kentucky was into a lot of power lifting. We were just the opposite. When we came in, we wanted our guys to be "lean, mean, running, hitting machines." We do the hang clean. We want our guys to be really strong in that lift. We want them to be strong on squats. We skip a lot of rope. Our guys box every day. People don't realize how good of an athlete most boxers are. If you have a great boxer, he is usually a good athlete and is in good shape. The linebackers don't have any swim moves. Everything he does is an uppercut. That is called a rip by most football teams. We get the heavy punching bag, have someone to hold it, and get our linebackers working three-minute rounds punching that bag. They dance, bounce, and uppercut that bag. They begin to get the idea of the uppercut and rip. We work three, three-minute rounds. We do that two to three times a week.

Linebackers have to play with their hands up. We use the little speed punching bag for that idea. We work on running ropes, but not the conventional type. I don't like the ropes that look like ladders. All that does is teach them to run in a straight line. We use zigzag ropes. We make them longer. We want them about 10 feet in length. They go through these ropes at an angle. They zigzag through the ropes. Every movement is a cut. We go forward and backward.

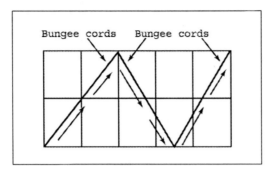

You don't ever want a linebacker playing with a flat foot. If they play flat-footed, you can hear their feet hitting the ground. They can easily get knocked off balance. We want them playing up on the toes.

We have a chute that is five-and-a-half feet tall. We train our linebackers under it. At the University of Kentucky, we have a factory-made one. I built mine at Valdosta State. I built it out of two-by-sixes and chicken wire. We set three cones underneath the chute and the coach stands on the side. The linebackers line up on the cones. The kids straddle the cones. They get in a good stance. We make them use a read step to start with. From there, we go to a counter step. In their stance, we want their feet inside their armpits. If the linebacker is stepping left, we want his right arm to come across like the rip move. That protects his outside kneecap so he can play with his hands. As he steps, we want him to get small so he can rip through. On the counter step, he has to step like a read step, then reverse and go the other way.

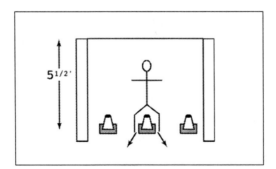

The next thing is our pass-drop drill. If the linebacker makes the first step right on his pass drop, he is in great shape. Our linebackers, as they read dropback by the quarterback, always step up. They step up at a 45-degree step. We step up to get into the lane of the tight end running the drag route. From there, we can make the cut out to the drop area. We don't want to drop and have to retrace to come back under the drag. If we can take care of releases and get position on a receiver, you will cut down on passes by the underneath coverage. If the linebackers overdrop, the tight end has a free release under them. If the linebackers step up, it takes away the free release and it causes problems for the quarterback, because it makes his read harder. We work on this under the cage also. It is kind of opposite of what people have been saying.

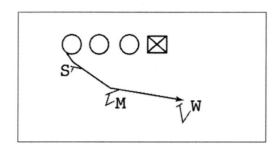

After that, we go to the one-man sled and work on defeating a blocker. I never want my guys taking on a whole blocker. We play with the thumbs up. If the palms are down, it is easy to knock your arms down. With the thumbs up, it is hard. We want the arm inside the frame of the body. When they throw a blow, it is inside their framework. The feet are the most important thing in defeating a block. If the foot is not in a correct fit, it doesn't matter what happens with the hands and arms. The most important thing is to work on the steps. We want our inside foot up. When the linebacker's hips get even with the blocker's hips is when the rip comes. If they throw too early, they'll get tangled with the blocker.

If we are going to punch up on the blocker, we set right in the center of him. The linebacker plants his feet and drives up. I put a jersey on the one-man sled dummy. We never want to hit the top of the numbers on the dummy's jersey. We want to tag the dummy with our fist on the lower part of the number and right in the sternum. We don't play with our hands. We try to make him spit blood. The outside arm is used as a club. We punch with the inside fist and club with the outside arm.

It is not a perfect world. Sometimes the blocker gets out in front of the linebacker. The blocker gets position on the linebacker. If the blocker gets too far in front, we backdoor the play. If we get the overplay, we fit into the blocker and backdoor the play. That is the counter step we did underneath the cage. We do these drills every day.

The next thing we do is a one-man tackling drill. We don't go live in our tackling drills. I learned this from Bum Phillips the year I worked with him at the Oilers. If your guys get real good on tackling a dead target, they will be good tacklers. You have to build confidence and get him into the right position. If during the learning process, your tackler is having to adjust and change his technique to full-speed ballcarriers, the tackler never gets the consistent way to tackle. He has to change all the time for the speed of the guy he is going against in practice. The dummy is always going to be the same. We put jerseys on all the dummies so we can check head placement. We go through face-up tackling and across-the-bow tackling. We never risk injury in practice by doing it this way. Since we've been at Kentucky, we've had seven injuries in practice. We've had four ankles, two shoulders, and one thumb injury. Five of those have been on the offensive end. We don't hurt our people, so we can take them to games. There is nowhere on our schedule where it says UK vs. UK. I've heard all the comments about how we don't hit enough. I think our kids will hit with anyone.

If you can only do one drill, this is the one you want to do. We line up an offensive lineman, fullback, and tailback. The linebacker takes on the offensive lineman running at an angle outside. He takes him on with his inside foot up and rips across. He next encounters the fullback and does the same thing. He takes him on with his inside foot up and rips through. Then he tackles the tailback with an across-the-bow tackle with his outside foot up. If he makes the tackle with his inside foot up, it will be an arm tackle. He has to get the outside foot up, head across the body, and shoulder into the body. That is our warm-up.

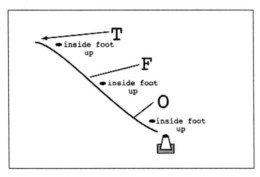

After the warm-up, we go to a read drill. I put the Mike and Sam linebacker in the drill. They play the isolation play. We play the iso a little bit different than a lot of people. The fullback comes through the dummies and blocks. The tailback takes an open step and can go anywhere he wants, as long as he goes through the dummies. On the *iso Sam*, the Sam linebacker is coming 1,000 miles an hour—or as fast as he can come. He puts his outside shoulder on the inside hip of the fullback and gets square and as deep as he can. The Mike linebacker rips across and gets square to the outside of the Sam linebacker. We are dictating where the football can go. We are not going to leave any room for the tailback to cut anywhere except where we are playing. Our kids are going to know where the cut is going to take place. The Willie linebacker is running

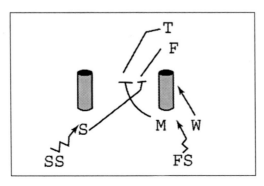

through the A gap. He is not shuffling behind the line. The strong and weak safeties are coming up to fill front and backside. We play nine guys on the line of scrimmage with one tight end and two backs in the backfield.

The *iso Mike* is the most dangerous of the iso reads. The Mike linebacker is responsible for the inside A gap. He takes his outside pad and drives up on the fullback as deep as he can get. He takes his inside hip. As soon as the Sam linebacker sees that play, he runs through the top part of the A gap. The down tackle is outside for the outside cut with the strong safety coming up in that position also. The free safety is coming up on the other side for the cut back.

On the *iso Willie*, we play it like the iso Sam. The Willie linebacker comes hard on the fullback. He takes him deep with his outside shoulder on the fullback's inside hip. He squares up at that point. The Mike linebacker comes over the Willie linebacker and fits outside to make the tackle. The Sam linebacker runs through the backside A gap. The strong safety comes up outside the Sam linebacker looking for the cutback. That is one way we play it.

We can call the box technique. If we do that, the Willie linebacker takes on the fullback with his inside shoulder and squares up. That forces the ball back inside and that is where the Mike linebacker is coming. We can box to the Sam side also.

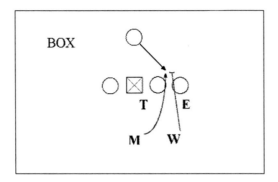

Let's go to the trap. Anytime the fullback steps toward the waxed guard, they are going to run the trap. When the Mike linebacker reads that move, he comes humming. He runs as tight to the center as he can. He is going to wreck the trap right there. The down tackle tries to get square, because the ball is going to bounce outside. We always have an alternate plan to go to. If we let the tackle come down and wrong-arm the trap, that is called *tag*. The Mike linebacker rips across and fits outside. It is easy to see the difference between the iso read and the tight trap read on the fullback. Here is a coaching point for you. Don't ever coach your linebackers from behind the defense. Get behind the offense, where you can see their techniques, eyes, and what they are looking at.

A linebacker corps that is setting and waiting to make tackles is going to give up a lot of long runs by the tailback. We want our linebackers on the move. Once the Mike linebacker hits the A gap on the trap, he wants to get square. We don't want him to continue outside on an angle. You can run these drills against bags if you want to. We work an awful lot of half-line drills to get the look we want.

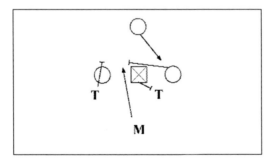

The next thing we have to play is the counter. To play the counter to the weakside, the linebackers have to know where their help is. The defensive end turns his shoulders and runs hard toward the B gap. He wants to collision the guard with a wrong-arm technique. He puts his outside shoulder on the inside hip of the pulling guard, between the knee and thigh pad. He puts his foot in the middle of the pulling guard's crotch and rips through him. What we want him to do is take the pulling guard and tackle out. The Willie linebacker replaces the defensive end and penetrates at least a yard deep in the backfield. If the defensive end was not successful in taking both the guard and tackle out of the play, the Willie linebacker has to take the tackle on.

The Mike linebacker plays over the top of the offensive tackle. He fills outside and his fit should be outside of the Willie linebacker. The Willie linebacker can wrong-arm and make a ton of tackles. We can also box this play. The Willie takes the tackle on with his inside shoulder. The Mike linebacker runs through the B gap and makes the stick as the back cuts up. We always want to have more than one way to play a play.

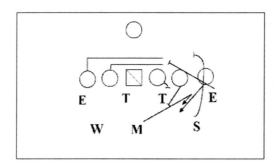

If we have the counter-gap play to the strongside, it is basically the same play except for the Mike linebacker. As the Mike linebacker pursues, he can go over the top of the tackle's block, but never over the block of the tight end. He goes over the tackle's block and fits right in the C gap. This helps the Mike linebacker on the bootleg off this play. As he flows over the tackle, he picks up the tight end. When he sees the tight end not blocking, he wheels and pins the tight end. He runs with the tight end across the field.

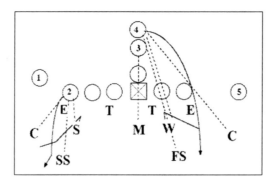

That is how we play the iso, trap, and counter gap from the I formation. If we get a king or queen set, we crosskey it. A king set is the fullback-off set in the halfback position to the tight end side. The queen set is the opposite, with the fullback to the split end side. The Mike linebacker keys the tailback and the Sam and Willie linebackers crosskey. Anything that comes away from the fullback is going to take some time to get back.

I want to get into some coverage for the linebackers. If I were coaching in high school, there is only one coverage I would play. We call it *read*. We number the receivers starting with the flanker to the strongside. The flanker is 1, the tight end is 2, the fullback is 3, the tailback is 4, and the split end is 5. The reason we don't number them 1 and 2 strong and weak is for communication purposes. If my guy comes off the field and tells me number 4, I know it is the weak inside receiver. The Sam linebacker, strong safety, and strong corner are reading number 2. On the weakside, Willie, the weak safety, and the weak corner are reading number 4. The Mike linebacker is reading 3 by himself.

If the tight end releases vertically, the Sam linebacker steps up, takes a 45-degree angle, and drives to the tight end's inside hip. He plays a wall-off technique until he gets to a release point, where he releases him to the strong safety. After he releases him to the strong safety, he takes another 45-degree angle and settles up. The Sam linebacker has to be between the receiver and the quarterback. He has help over the top. The Willie linebacker plays the same technique on number 4 coming vertically weak.

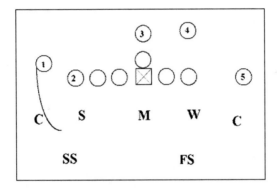

If 2 runs a shoot route, which is a short flat, he is in the no-cover zone. The Sam linebacker lets him go and drives at a 45-degree angle looking for number 1. He is looking to take away the curl from number 1. Don't look at the quarterback. I tell my guys the quarterback will never catch the football if he is throwing it. Why look at him? He is going to lie to you anyway. The linebacker wants to get between the receiver and

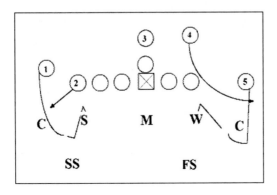

quarterback in the throwing lane. He has help over the top, and the corner is taking the shoot route if it gets deeper. All we are doing is converting coverage according to what the routes are. To the weakside, the Willie linebacker does the same thing based on what number 4 does. If he comes out on the shoot, the Willie linebacker breaks on a 45 for the split end on the curl.

The only other thing number 2 can do is run the drag. The Sam linebacker steps up, comes out at a 45-degree angle, collisions the tight end, and makes him work to get into the pattern. He tries to flatten the tight end and make him go underneath. He drives the 45-degree angle, again looking for a curl pattern. If there is nothing coming, he settles up, looking inside for something coming from the other side. If there is a curl, he drives to the curl and gets under the receiver's hip.

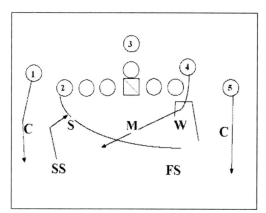 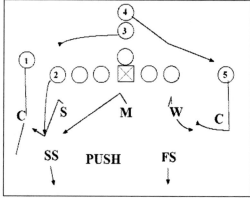

The Mike linebacker always goes with the number 3. If the number 3 receiver goes strong on a flare route, the Mike linebacker steps up, opens on a 45-degree angle, and drives into the strong hook area. If the Mike linebacker doesn't think he can get to the number 3 receiver, he calls "push" and replaces the Sam linebacker. The Sam linebacker moves outside and takes the number 3 receiver. We are 4-on-3 to the strongside and 3-on-2 to the weakside.

If we move a linebacker outside in coverage, the other linebacker moves a half a man toward him. The Mike linebacker is lined up so he can cover the outside shoulder of 3. He is playing the run first, but as soon as the quarterback gets off the ball, he is going to pass coverage. Willie is taking the zigzag motion. That is motion toward the quarterback and coming back to his original alignment. The worst thing that Willie can do is keep moving. They are looking for Willie to get out of position in an outside alignment. Anytime we get motion, we set with our cleats in the ground. Willie still has outside leverage on the run and the motion man has to get outside of the Willie to get a release, which is what we want him to do anyway.

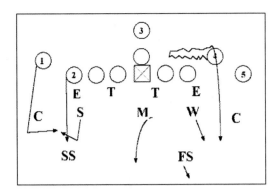

If we get two tight ends and two flankers with one back, we look at the depth of the one back. If he is three to five yards deep, he is a fullback. If the back is seven yards deep, he is a tailback. If the back is seven yards deep, you won't get much inside zone plays. Everything will go outside. If he is three to five yards, you can expect some inside zone plays, a block on a pass play, or some inside core play between the tackles. The linebacker has to know that.

We have two or three things we do. The first thing we do is called *Lincoln*. That pushes the left fieldside end down into a 5 technique. The tackle moves to a strong shade of the center. The weak tackle goes to a 3 technique and the weak end goes to a 9 technique. The Sam linebacker moves outside to foot level with the defensive linemen in a 90 technique. This is an ability adjustment. The better he is, the tighter we can play him. You adjust him vertically and horizontally according to his ability. The Mike linebacker moves over to a 3 technique strong. The Willie linebacker comes to a 3 stack on the backside. The route you have to cover is four verticals. You must stay two deep. You can't go three deep. All you have to do is tell the safeties if they get the block down by the tight ends, they are committed to the run. That gives us nine guys on the run and the corners are out there on that island playing man. One mistake we made on defense this year was we played our corners too soft. That gave the offense the quick ball when they needed it. This year we are going to play "Saturday night in the parking lot." That means they are going to have to fight their asses off that line. We are going to play hard corners and get aggressive.

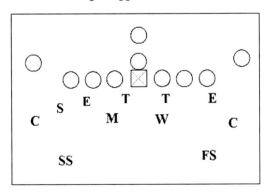

If the back is seven yards deep, our corners will be back at six yards, because we know it will be a pass or outside cut. If the back is at three yards, they will get tighter than three yards of dirt. We are still playing read coverage. The reads are the same. Once a kid understands that, he can communicate with you. He is not dropping out to some spot. He is covering a route.

We key a lot of things. In the shotgun set, if the quarterback is in front of the two backs, that is a draw set. If he's on the same level or behind the two backs, that is a pass set. Our kids look for those kinds of things. We try to find the little clues and hints in film study and game situations to give our kids the edge. We practice all kinds of different sets and schemes. That's why we don't get upset if our opponent comes out with something he hasn't been using. We practice against everything and have plans to counter anything we see. We practice the whole menu and refine it into what we have to stop. We practice against about four running plays and four pass plays. That is all we cue them up on. We only defense first-and-10 and third-and-medium. The opponent will always go to his bread-and-butter on those downs.

You can usually go by the zone your opponent is in. They usually have some philosophy about going in or coming out. Usually, between the 40-yard lines people are pretty wide open. The closer they get to the goal line, the more conservative most offensive coaches get. They go to two and three backs or two tight ends. They jam it all up in there. The guy I worry about is the guy who spreads you all over the place. They take away all the defense's leverage points and open up creases you can't cover.

I don't worry about a guy who is a 50-50 balanced team. He runs it 50 percent of the time and throws it 50 percent of the time. They can't make up their minds whether to run or pass the ball. The guys I worry about are guys like Hal Mumme, who throw it about 80 percent of the time. A team that runs the option about 90 percent of the time will give you fits. They know what they are doing. It doesn't matter what adjustments you make, they have something else to go with in their scheme. They are committed to that part of the game.

If you guys want to come up and see us, we work at 6:00 a.m. We work the defense on form running on Monday and Wednesday. On Tuesday, we do agilities in the morning. On Fridays, we have P.T.A day. That stands for pain, torture, and agony. We have a circuit in the weight room that they go through. We tell our guys that those guys over at Knoxville are sleeping this time of the morning. We tell them the guys at Gainesville are probably getting in from a party. We are up here working and that is going to give us the edge. We are better workers and more focused. That is the way we look at it. Gentlemen, I've enjoyed it. You all come see us.

9

Outside Linebacker Pass Rush Techniques

Bobby Morrison
University of Michigan
1994

Outside linebacker is a position we are having a hard time finding good people to play. We are looking for a player that can defend the run over a tight end, and we are looking for a player that can drop in the pass coverage and play pass defense. We are looking for a player that can play man-to-man on a tight end or on a wide receiver.

The two areas I want to discuss today concern defending the pass and the pass rush. The latter is probably the most undercoached area in the game. The premium in the NFL today is to find that great pass rusher. We are seeing more passing formations in college today. Ten or fifteen years ago, everyone ran the ball. It was a running game in college. Pass rush was not emphasized that much. Today it is being given special emphasis. We try to give it special emphasis in our defensive scheme. Most of you will agree—at least the secondary coaches will agree—the best way to have great pass coverage is to have a great pass rush. The number one way to play pass defense is to have constant pass pressure. We put a special emphasis on our pass rush. Here are some things we do to give it special emphasis. If you want your pass rush to improve, you must give it emphasis.

At Michigan, we have a defensive production board. The number one way to score points on the production board is to score a touchdown. The second highest way to score a point is on a sack. That tells you how much we think about a pass rush. The next point is to apply pressure, and the next is to force the quarterback to hurry his throw. Those are the things we stress. We stress the sack, pressure, and a hurry.

When we work in pads against our offense, we want to get the work against the pass. When we are in a scrimmage and we rush the quarterback and can sack him, we touch him or tag him on the hips or rear end and call out "sack." The quarterback can still throw the ball. This gives us a chance to work against the pass. Now, this upsets the offensive team and the coaches when they hear us call out the "sack." This lets them know we are going to emphasize the sacks.

We have a sack board in the hall. We put the player's picture up when he gets a sack. On the sack board, we go from 1-25 and 26-50. Then we have our 11 games across the top. If we get two sacks in the first game, in the first slot would be one kid's picture, and in the second slot would be the second kid's picture. If we go a game and do not get a sack, we do not have anyone in that slot. If we get four sacks in the next game, then we have four pictures. It is another way of emphasizing sacks.

In the NFL, there may be 25 or 30 different pass rush techniques. I would say on the college level we are talking about 10 to 20 pass rush techniques. This includes games and individual techniques. The best way to find out about your players as far as rushing the quarterback is to do this. Find out who your best pass rush players are and then ask them what they think they can use to beat the blocker to get the sack. Ask him what pass rush he has confidence in. Work with each player until they have two or three good pass rush techniques. Now, we work on more than that. You should work until you can master two or three good techniques. After you master two or three pass rush techniques, then work on the counters for those techniques.

We break pass rush down into three phases. The first phase is the mental phase. This includes down-and-distance, tendencies, and game plan. I have to know, if it is third-and-long, what are the passing situations? What is the game plan against this offense? Do we want to rush the quarterback more than we play the run? What are we going to do on defense this week? What tendencies do they have when they are in certain formations? That is the first thing we determine. The next thing, we study films. Who gives away the pass? You have more time to watch the film than the players do. You have to study the offensive blockers. You can find someone along the line that will indicate the play is going to be a pass. The next thing we want to teach our players is how they are going to get blocked on each type of play. You have to tell the players how they are going to block when they throw the pass. They must know who is going to block them. You have to explain to the kids what is going to happen to them on the blocks.

The next phase is the physical phase. We must communicate to the rest of the front. If you read pass, you have to be able to communicate this to the rest of the team. The communication is the first step in the physical phase. Get on the edge. When we know it is a pass, we want to get on the edge of the blocker. We do not want to be head up on the blocker. If you are head up and you read pass, you want to get on the edge of the blocker. Change your key from the man to the ball. We look at the ball so it will give us a better chance to get off on the snap. I want us to be called offsides about three out of five times in spring practice. I want it to be called. I want to emphasize to them how tight they have to get on the football. If you will go back and look at the film, you can see a lot of times when mistakes are made, the player was not up on the ball far enough. We are not going to get much pressure if the man is not up on the ball. Talk to them about being offsides. We can have all four down linemen over the ball by six inches and the officials will not call offsides; all four of them are offsides. But you let one man be one inch over the ball and the other three be back, and the officials will call offsides. I have seen it happen. If you get them all up there, they have a reluctance to call all of them offsides. Get as much of the ball as you can.

The next thing we are going to do is to change our stance. When we are in a run stance, we are basically in a heel-toe relationship. Now, when it is pass, we want to kick back our backside foot six to twelve inches. We want to get in a sprinter's stance. We want a heel-toe and run. We want to narrow the base of our feet, and our feet are outside our shoulders. We want to move the hand up a little. We get the hand up as far as we can and we get the tail up in the air. When we read pass, we elongate our stance and get more weight on our hand so we can come off the ball.

The third phase is our techniques. We break them down into speed and speed rushes, power, and finesse. We have three types of techniques. I will just hit on a few of them today. I can't cover all of the techniques, because of time. We have kids that can only do one or two of these techniques. We only want them to do those techniques they feel confident they can do successfully. Whatever the kid can do best is what you want the kid to do. The next step is to go to the counters after he gets two or three techniques down.

Under our speed rushes, we have a speed club and rip. We have a speed club and arm over. We have our counter step club and rip. Included in our power rushes are the bull rush, a bull rush with the hand, a stab technique, and a butt-and-flip technique. I will tell them to butt and flip the arm over, butt and flip with a rip, and then we go into finesse moves. The finesse moves are basically stunts. We are going to change up the rush lanes with different people. You cannot consider foot and head fakes as finesse moves. We incorporate them right in with our regular rushes. Those are a part of our speed, power, and finesse rushes.

Where do we start? Basically, we start on pass rush in our winter program. Many of you do it in your summer conditioning programs. This is a drill we use to start with. We call it the duck-goose drill. We ended up running this drill with our defensive linemen and outside linebackers. The drill is so good, everyone does the drill in our winter program.

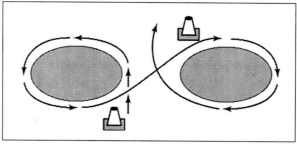

Duck-goose drill

We take a rope that is about one inch in diameter, and make two circles with the rope that are 10 feet in diameter. They are the same size as a center jump circle in basketball. You do not want too big of a rope. The one-inch rope is big enough, or a garden hose is good enough. We want to teach the players to run in nonparallel lines. When we run most of our drills, we run on straight lines. The big emphasis here is to run in nonparallel lines. The ropes are about five yards apart. We start at the cone with a player on the left and have him run around the rope or hose. He goes from one circle to the other circle and finishes at the second cone. Once we get good at that, we have a second player chase the first player. It becomes competitive. We tell the second man to catch the man and pass him if he can. The big thing in running in nonparallel lines is the body lean in turning the corners, and keeping the shoulder dipped to the inside. Some kids are so stiff you would think you will need to take an oilcan on the field for them. Some kids make it look easy because it is just natural for them. They can pass inside or outside on the run.

Our next drill is what we call a *get off drill*. We do this drill every day as the outside linebackers come on the field. We take a green football and have cones set up seven yards deep. We have a manager at seven yards. We use a green ball just because it blends in with the grass and it makes the defensive man concentrate more. It is a get-off-the-ball drill, but we call it the green ball drill. We painted the ball green. I get them in a stance and start calling the cadence. I remind them they are to move on the ball. I will talk to them about their stance, and what they must do when the ball is snapped. "Set, go, down, ready." I snap the ball and they do not move. Then I get on them and tell them they must move on the ball. I want to make sure they are concentrating on

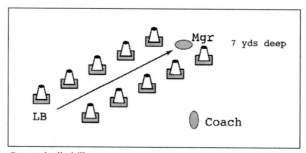

Green ball drill

the snap. The first thing we do is to go about one-quarter speed coming off the ball. We want the outside linebacker to go to the manager, who is seven yards deep. That is where we think a five-step drop quarterback will set his feet. The angle we use is the angle we want the outside linebacker rushing in. We will change the angle at times. We want to get on the edge and run the corner.

Next, the manager will have a ball and he will raise the ball up in the air. As the linebacker comes to the manager, he will rake the backside arm with the hand. The manager raises the ball up and we knock it out of his hand. The next part of the drill is to have the linebacker recover the fumble. We work on the drill from both sides. That is our green ball, get off drill. We start each practice with this drill.

When we talk about a speed rush, we start basically with a drill where we talk about points. We have an offensive lineman and a quarterback at seven yards deep. We put the blocker down with a football. The set point for the offensive lineman is this. It is about one yard inside and four yards deep. That is where the offensive lineman is going to make contact with the outside linebacker. It is one yard inside and about four yards deep. That is the set point. That is where the offensive coaches want to make sure the blocker has his shoulders square.

The first thing we do in teaching the speed rush is to have the linebacker get off the ball without the offensive lineman. Now we have a blocker on the drill. The goal for the pass rush is to sack the quarterback, to force him to hurry his throw, or to pressure him. The objective of a pass rush is to get the offensive blocker's shoulders turned. We must get the offensive blocker's shoulders turned. When I see pro scouts come in and test our players, the thing they want to see, when you have a wide rusher like an outside linebacker, is if that tackle can get to the set point of four yards with his shoulders still square. If you can't do that as an offensive tackle, you can't play in the NFL. They will have a hard time protecting against the hard corner rush. Knowing this, we try to get that tackle to turn his shoulders. That is our objective. There are a couple of ways of doing this. Speed is the first way to do that, and alignment is number two. Speed and alignment will make that tackle turn his shoulders.

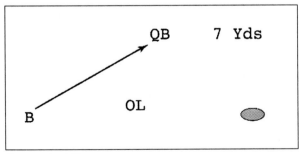

Pass rush drill

We timed the drill to see how fast we were on defense. It takes the outside linebacker about 1.4 to 1.6 seconds to get back to the quarterback without a blocker in front of him. Quarterbacks that use a five-step drop go back about seven yards deep. If they throw on time, they are throwing at 2.5 seconds. If the defensive man can get there in 1.5 and the quarterback throws it in 2.5, then we have 1.0 seconds to beat the blocker. You can forget all of the shaking and baking at the line. It is a time factor. If the ball is thrown at 2.5 and you run the rush in 1.5, you only have 1.0 seconds to beat the man. You can't screw around on the line of scrimmage.

We start our basic pass rush from a run stance. A run rush stance is different than a pass rush stance. When it is second-down-and-long, or third-and-long, we want you in a pass rush stance and we want you to come off the ball like a snake. We associate the move like a cobra ready to strike. When the ball is snapped, we are coming. We take the offensive lineman and sit him on the line and work against him with the speed rush. The offensive lineman does not move.

The next thing we do is to have the offensive lineman come out of his stance one yard. Still, we have no contact. All we are trying to do is to let the defender know what it is like. The blocker works outside, but again, we do not have to have any contact on the drill. Next, we start to use a close down drill. We take the offensive lineman and set him on the line. We snap the ball and have the lineman make his move for one yard. Now, we have the linebacker come across and touch the blocker with his hands. We want to get on him as fast as we can. If you are going to make a move on the blocker, you can't make it a yard away from him.

The next thing is to move the blocker back two yards. Now the ball is snapped and the blocker goes back two yards and sets. The linebacker comes off the ball and explodes to the blocker and puts his hands on him. There is no real contact, just the hands. Next, we have the blocker back up three yards. It gets very hard for the linebacker to get to the blocker to put his hands on the blocker. He has to explode to get there. If the linebacker can get his hands on the blocker before he can get to five yards deep, he is a good pass rusher. You may want to find out how many players you have that can do that. You must get close to the blocker before you can execute any kind of move. That is what the close down drill does. It teaches them to close down the distance and to get to the blocker.

The next thing we do is go to our hand drills. They can do these drills while they are standing around. The objective is to get the blocker's shoulders turned. The blocker has his hands on you and you want to work to get his hands off you. The first drill we use is a double-slap hands down. If he has his hands inside on me, this is what I do. Double-slap hands down. We want to get the hands off. We do three of those in a row. Next, we use a crossclub. We get the arm the blocker uses the best and crossclub that arm. We get this from the film and the scouting report. Then we do the inside club. We use the hands inside when we think it is a run. These are things we use to get the blocker's hands off us. Another thing we can use is the elbow snap and arm over. If you do not know it is a pass and you played the run, you can use the elbow snap and arm over. They can work on these in the gym class.

What do you do when you are even with the blocker? This comes into play when you start talking about the pass rush. We tell them this is the time they must burst to the quarterback. There is a burst that comes into play. Once he gets even with the blocker, there has to be a burst to the quarterback. Once they get even with the blocker, they must not stop. They must have that burst. When you finish up a drill, teach them to burst at the end of the drill toward the quarterback.

I want to take one basic pass rush and talk about the counters that we use on them. Let's take the speed rush. First of all, because of the angle we have our players align in the three-step passing game, which is fire-out-and-chop, we can go underneath the block. We can see the block. They are wider and can see the chop block on the three-step drop pass. We go under the chop block. We take one step and come underneath the man. We are talking about a speed rush where we want to get to the set point. Let me cover a couple of counters we use on the speed rush on the rip. If we have a rip move sunk in and the blocker's hand is up in the air, we want to push the hand up in the air, and step through. If we feel the arm is high, we push up and step through. If we rip and sink the move and the blocker is a little lower, we want to pull the rip out and go to the arm over. We use those two counters for the rip move.

When you get to the four-yard set point, you must make a decision. At that point, do you keep taking the edge at the quarterback because you have the blocker's shoulders turned? Or, do you have to make a counter move at that point on the blocker? A couple of things we do will help. If we feel he is pushing up outside and we are too wide, we can do two things. If we are going to spin, we want to feel pressure from the backside arm. If we feel pressure from the backside arm, the spin is good. If we do not feel pressure from the backside arm, then the spin is no good. If there is no pressure and you spin, he comes back on you. If you have pressure from the backside arm, you can use his momentum to come around the corner.

The other thing we do is to use what we call a *hump move*. If I feel I am getting too wide, I want to take the inside arm and put it underneath the blocker's inside arm and lift him up and pull him toward me. I want to pull him toward me and come back inside. If you feel yourself getting too wide, and you feel pressure on the backside, use the spin move. We take the outside arm and come around and put it in the center of his back. We come around and we always finish it with the rip. We try to finish every technique we have with a rip technique to keep the blocker off us. If we do not feel pressure, we take the inside arm and put it under his inside arm and lift him over on the hump move. We come underneath and then finish up with the rip move. That is feeling yourself getting pushed too wide. Those are the basic counters we have for the speed rush. The speed rush is not a great technique. It is speed, speed. If it is a speed rush, you still must have the counters off them.

If you have any left-handed players, you may want to do this. It is better fundamentally if you are on the right side if you are in a left-hand stance, and the guy on the left-hand side is in a right-hand stance. We do not do this all of the time because we do not have many left-handed players. You are fundamentally sounder against the run and the pass like this. We do not make a big stink about it because the most important thing is to have players that get off the ball.

When we close on the quarterback, we do not put our hands up in the air until the frontside hand comes off the ball. I do not want players running after the quarterback with their hands up in the air. When the frontside hand of the quarterback comes off the ball, then we can go up in the air. Our landmark is the backside shoulder of the quarterback. We do not want the quarterback to break containment outside. We go for the backside shoulder.

An example of a power rush would be a bull rush. A bull rush is where we come off the ball and we want to get the blocker's head to snap. If we can find a blocker that is on his heels in pass protection, then we will use the bull rush against him. You can do different things on down-and-distance. You can tell the linebacker on first-and-10 that if he gets to the blocker he will have to use the bull rush. A bull rush on second- or third-and-long is an absolute change-up. That is not what you want to do. It would be a change of pace for the offensive blocker. The bull rush can be used early in the game to let the offense know they are in for a hard game.

The most important thing about the bull rush is that you hit the blocker with the heel of the helmet under the chin and get the hands under him. It is a three-point explosion into the blocker. You do not want to expose your chest. You need the three-point contact. You can feel him backing up. Sooner or later he will stand his ground. If he is soft, we can take him back to the quarterback. If he stands and fights, we want to hit the bull rush on the edge. We do not want to hit it down the middle. Unless the man is soft, we do not want to hit it down the middle. We want it on the edge. We want it on the peck. We butt with the head and the hands, but we continue to work on the edge.

We may hit the blocker and he is soft and he sits down. We will club with the outside arm and work to get to the edge. We club and flip. When you club and get the man off you, we flip the hips. We bull rush, then club, and flip the hips. Now, I can go arm over or rip. We want to get the hip away from the blocker.

The last move is the stab. You will see these on tape later. Pass rushers that have long arms have a better chance on the rush. We butt the blocker and grab the man by the throat. You can use one arm a lot better than two. The rusher takes the man by the throat. That is what we call the stab. We may grab them by the jersey, but it still is a stab. That is used for players that do not have a lot of speed.

Foot fakes and head fakes can all be included in speed rushes, power rushes, or in the finesse category. We want to study the offensive tackle and figure out how he is setting. If the defender widens and the offensive tackle jumps out after him, I have a chance to club and rip him and come back inside underneath. If we get a blocker that is setting short on the line of scrimmage, or tight to the line and does not get off the line, basically we are going to use a foot fake and rip and come outside and use the arm over move. Head fakes and foot fakes do not require a lot of finesse. When you coach these fakes, make sure they are always making progress toward the quarterback when they are doing it. They can't beat the man at the line of scrimmage. Everything must be pointed toward the quarterback. If we step inside with a foot fake, it has to be going toward the quarterback. It is the same with the head fake to the outside. We want to be upfield toward the quarterback and gaining ground and come back inside. You must gain depth to the quarterback.

The finesse games are the games you can get into with down linemen. If you have two offensive linemen that are setting inside and protecting, then you have to do something to get these two on different levels so you can create a pass rush lane. If you let the two sit inside and pass block, they will sit there all day. You must get them on different levels to create pass rush lanes. You must create separation in the blockers. We do that with finesse games or stunts.

The reason we use them is twofold. First, you must change up the pass rush lanes against the team you are playing, unless you think the coaching staff does not study football. If you rush the same way all the time, they can block you. If you can change up the pass rush lanes, and use the finesse games, they can't sit and wait for you. Those games are what the offense does not want to see. It takes a lot of their time preparing against them. That is almost a base for us. We start on this part of our game from day one.

Before I go to the videotape, I want to highlight a few points. First is the stance. Get the weight forward and more than a heel-toe relationship. Take short kick steps, six to twelve inches. Get the tail up in the air. Don't put your free arm on your knee. We are almost in a 3.5-point stance. My hand is not on the knee. We want a free arm. That is why we call it a 3.5 stance.

We want to get the blocker's hands off us. We use the different techniques to get his hands off us. When we get even with the blocker, we want to burst to the quarterback. The landmark to the quarterback is the upfield number. If the quarterback takes his front hand off the ball, you get the hands up. It is important to turn and chase the ball after it is released by the quarterback. This is something you cannot coach enough. Turn and chase the ball. We want them to turn and run downfield and strip the ball. You have to emphasize it over and over.

We have a no-free-lunch technique. There is no such thing as a free lunch. We line a man up in a stance and have him come off the ball as hard as he can. We have a cone set up downfield. We have the blocker take one step and then I will call "go." The linebacker takes one step and when he hears me call "go" he must turn and run to the cone downfield. This tells him that someone is going to block him all the time. *There is no free lunch*. You may let the blocker go two steps before you call "go." The "go" is to let the linebacker know he is too far upfield and he needs to get downfield. This is what we call *retrace your steps*.

I want to show the tape to let you see these moves. Thank you.

10

Linebacker Play and Defensive Fronts

Fred Pagac
The Ohio State University
1999

The first thing I want to do is go over our basic philosophy and talk about some of the defenses we run at Ohio State. I have some film later on to show you on our packages. If you have any questions while I'm talking, just sound off.

When you start coaching, you have to develop a coaching philosophy. Besides teaching the basic fundamentals like tackling, pursuing, and defeating blocks, there are other things to consider. We want to teach the scheme, responsibilities, strengths, and weaknesses of the defense, where the help is, and presnap keys.

The second thing we deal with is our players' philosophy. The things that we have always talked about are stopping the run and having an attitude. We want to be confident and aggressive. In spring practice, we start talking about the next play. The meaning behind that is that every time the ball is snapped, we want our kids giving great effort. Don't get caught up in the mental aspect of worrying about not making the last play. If something bad happens, screw it. Let's play hard the next play. You will not see us ripping their butts on the sideline for making mistakes. We may get on them if they don't hustle or lack discipline, but never for making mistakes. In our meeting, we talk about HEAP. That stands for hustle, emotion, attitude, and physical. We want them to play hard and play fast. If they play hard and fast, we say that we have 11 silver bullets on the field.

We have a linebacker philosophy at Ohio State. Our base philosophy is to make opponents beat us left-handed. Most opponents have strengths and weaknesses. There are very few opponents who you have to defend equally. Most teams either run the ball better than they throw or throw it better than they run it. Stop what that team does the best, and make them beat you with the other part of their game. Most teams we play want to establish the running game to open up their passing game. We feel that if we control the running game and force them into a passing situation, we have the advantage.

We talk about stopping the run on run downs and reacting to the pass. We want to be gap sound in every defense we run. It doesn't matter whether it is one- or two-gap defense. We want to be strong in the middle against the run and pass. If we are going to get beat, it will be with the outside running game. Do not give up the line of scrimmage to the cutback play. In the passing game, we are going to give up the outside throw. We never want the ball thrown down the middle.

We want to get an extra hat to where the ball is. Last year, we gave up 67 yards a game rushing. That led the nation in rushing defense. Our leading tacklers were our Buck and Will linebackers and our strong safety. It wasn't our Mike linebacker, as you might think. To get the extra hat to the ball, we choreograph that with the secondary and linebackers. We use a two- or three-deep scheme. When we have our inside run period, our safeties are always in that drill. We get into a lot of eight- and nine-man fronts.

If we need to stop the run, we will stunt some. We have a stunt package to move all four down linemen. When we run stunts, we are very gap sound. If we need to, we will blitz. I don't believe in blitzing to stop the run. If I do, then we are locked up on the tight end and both backs with our safeties and Will linebacker. That is the only way I blitz for penetration.

We are a multiple-front team that uses the KISS principle. Our linebackers play four different fronts, but they only have to learn two different techniques. Basically, they have to learn two sets of keys and techniques. I don't think that is too hard to learn. It is important to plug as few techniques as possible into your fronts.

We are basically an under team, which we call *tight*. It is a reduction to the weakside. We play an over package also. In our defense, we do not play a 9 technique with our defensive down people. In our 4-3 package, we have a 6 and 3 technique, and a 1 and 5 technique for our down people.

The first front I'll talk about is the tight with a field call. We play this a lot on first-and-10. About 30 percent of the time, we will be in a three-deep look in the secondary. That could be a three-deep or man-free. About 35 to 40 percent of the time, we will be in a two-deep look. If the ball were on the defense's right hash mark, we make a left call. With that call, we would have a 1 and 5 technique to the tight end side. To the weakside, we would be in 3 and 5 techniques. In the secondary, we can play covers 2, 4, and 6, which are our two-deep looks. We can play covers 3, 5, and 7, which are our three-deep looks. We can play man-free or man.

When we make a field call, we anchor the secondary guys. That means they stay where they are and do not flip-flop from side to side. We play with a field corner and a boundary corner, and generally, against a twin set, both corners are on the same side. They generally take the two wideouts all over the field. We set our front in a 1 and 5 technique to the field and put our drop linebacker into the field. When we line up in the tight defense, we always give the offense an umbrella look or four across the board in the secondary. This front versus the run last year gave up 2.1 yards per carry.

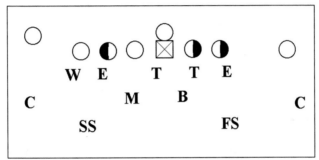

Under tight field defense

The next front we play is called *slide defense*. It is our stack package. Our linebackers for the most part are two-gap players. That means they have one gap on flow strong and one gap on flow weak. When we play this in a running downing situation, we like to play what we call *cover 4*. That puts both safeties into the run-support scheme. We basically play man-to-man outside, and our safeties and linebackers are in a read-run-support principle. In passing downs, we play cover 2, or we play cover 2 and blitz. When we line up in this defense, our presnap look is a cover 2 or 4 across-the-board look.

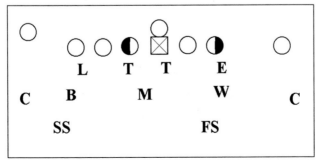

Slide defense

This next defense versus the running game gave up 1.7 yards per carry. We probably didn't play it enough. We only played it 52 times during the year. This was our *bear defense*. We want to give a presnap read of a man-free secondary. This defense is a five-man-go concept. When we get in this front, we can run the defense, use our blitz package, or use two-thirds zones. When we blitz, we don't blitz just to be blitzing. We blitz with a purpose in mind. If we know the type of pass protection we are facing, we use a blitz scheme that will be effective against that. What I like about this package is that we can get a four-man overload to the split end side and still have coverage to the tight end side. That is important to us.

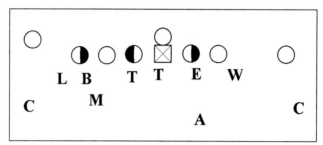

Bear defense

Those are the basic fronts we play. At Ohio State, we are fortunate to have kids who love to play the game. It is a good place for them to play also. They all hope they can make it to that next level. We have a 20-hour rule in college football, which includes the game. One thing that has helped us is our players coming in to watch film on their own.

We have some things that we say are linebacker musts. Some of these things I don't think you can teach. They either have it or they don't. But you can improve on them. There are traits that great linebackers have. Here are some of the traits they must have. They have to take control, show leadership, and gain respect. They must be able to communicate and have knowledge of the whole game. The most important thing they have to have is composure. They have to know total defense. They have to know the strengths and weaknesses of the defense. They have to know their responsibilities, where the extra hat is, and the support systems. They have to always keep the ball going east-west on the field.

Presnap keys are very important. We have to get eight people involved. Huddle calls and communication of automatics are important for the linebacker. The linebacker has to know the front, coverage, and what personnel are in the game. When we talk about personnel, we want to give our kids a menu. We have a number of personnel groupings. We flash these to our linebacker with signs. The 1-2 regular sign is for one tight end and two backs. If we have a 2-2 pair sign, there are two tight ends and two backs in the game. The 2-1 snake is for two tight ends and one back. The 1-1 viper sign is one tight end and one back. The 0-2 queen is no tight ends and two backs. The

0-1 shoot is no tight ends and one back. The linebacker has to know from combinations how many receivers are in the game. For instance, the 0-1 shoot has three wide receivers. Those types of things help the linebacker before we even break the huddle. If we have signed in a 2-2 call, the linebacker only has to watch for where the second type of end aligns.

By knowing what offensive groupings are in the game, the linebacker can anticipate types of formations, backfield sets, plays, and where the strength of the set may be. We always check the line split of the offensive linemen. If they widen, the play is probably coming inside. If they tighten, it is probably going outside. When the linebacker sees a wider gap in the B gap, he starts calling that to the defense. The receivers tell our secondary the same kinds of things with their splits. If the receiver tightens his split, it is probably because he is going to run the crossing pattern or crack on the linebacker. Anticipating will help the thought process of everyone on the defense.

The linebacker has to know his assignment, his alignment, and the adjustment to all his defenses. He has to know his keys. These are things that are taken care of in the presnap read of the linebacker. When the ball is snapped, he must react and execute. He must play with great effort. All that goes with playing hard and fast and being aggressive and confident. Football is a game of reaction.

I'm going to show you our tight defense with a reduction on the split end side. I'm going to show you our linebacker reads and secondary coverages that go with the defense. This defense is a tight-oriented front. The defense has two reads to it. We have a *read* or *cloud* call. The Mike linebacker makes his call depending on the set of the tight end. With the tight end left, we make a left call. That puts our nose tackle in a center shade to the tight end and our end in a 5 technique. Our presnap read tells us that we have regular personnel on the field. In our tight defense, we go to quarter-quarter cover in the secondary. When we talk about quarter-quarter, our strong safety and Will linebacker are reading the tight end's release or his block. The field corner has the Z receiver on his own. If he releases vertically, he has him with no help all over the football field.

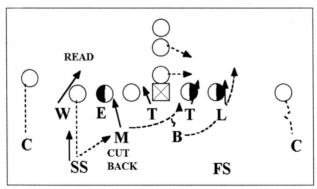

Tight read left

The front four have a gap assignment on alignment. We have a read support call to the left. That means the strong safety is involved in run support to the left side. The linebacker knows he has an extra hat to the left side. He wants to make sure that if he doesn't make the tackle, the ball goes outside to the left. It tells him that if he gets flow to his right, he can get moving because he has a cutback player behind him. If we were playing a cover 4, which means both safeties are in run support, the linebackers on movement would be in fast flow.

If we get a cloud call right, the Buck linebacker sees that he is on the split end side. He knows that in this coverage he has to become a slow football player. The cloud means the corner is rolling flat and the free safety is covering over the top of the corner. Therefore the Buck linebacker has to play the cutback on flow left because the free safety is gone. The same thing holds true for the Mike linebacker. If he gets isolation action at him, he has to spill the ball left. The Buck linebacker is playing slow for the cutback and is not filling strongside. If the Buck linebacker gets an isolation run to him, we are in good shape. The Buck linebacker can spill it to the outside, keeping his inside arm free. The Mike linebacker gets into a position behind his tackle where he can fast-flow outside the Leo end or rock back for a quick cutback. The strong safety has the cutback run. That is the tight defense with a two-deep principle.

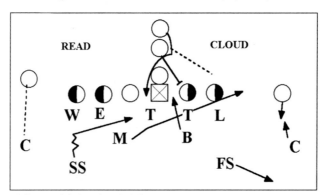

Tight read left—cloud right

I don't like to play tight cover 2 versus the running game. You have turned your linebackers into two-gap players all the time. They are going to be right about 50 to 60 percent of the time. The other 40 percent, the offense is going to get some big plays.

Our Will linebacker has an easy read but a hard technique. He is a 9 technique on the tight end. I am not a big supporter of guys in stances. He can move all over the place, but when the ball is snapped, he has to be in position and ready to play. The tight end tells him everything. If he gets a high hat, he plays pass. If he gets a down block, he plays the run. The Buck and Mike linebackers read the flow of the backfield. A tight flow is from the center to the outside hip of the guard. The Mike linebacker fills the B gap on tight flow. The Buck linebacker slow-plays, looking for the cutback. The strong safety reads the tight end and fills wherever he is needed.

The mid- to wide flow is from the outside hip of the tackle to outside wide. The Mike and Buck linebackers flow into a stack position on the end and strongside tackle. When the Mike linebacker gets to the stack position behind the end, he has beaten the guard's block. He has the ability to run through any gap that opens inside out to the ball. If no gap opens, he pursues the football along the line of scrimmage. Our safety is going to fit where he is needed, which generally is outside. Everyone is spilling the ball to him. Our normal alignment for our safeties is between nine and eleven yards. If we are in cover 6, at the snap of the ball, the strong safety should be about two yards outside the tight end and eight yards deep. I never want to see him aligned there. That is where he ends up. I want the quarterbacks and wideouts to read cover 2 in their presnap read. The split-flow action for the inside linebackers is the same as no flow. They play their gaps. Anytime the linebackers get a block from the fullback in the I or the setback, we spill the ball to the outside.

In our secondary calls, even numbers tell them it is some kind of two-deep principle. Odd numbers tell them it is some kind of three-deep principle. When we use colors, it is some kind of man coverage. When we talk about ZTF, which stands for *zone the formation*, we want to be in an eight-man front all the time, but we want the center field covered at all times. An example would be first-and-10 after we've had a fumble or interception by our offense. That is what we call a *sudden change*. It is an unexpected change of position, which throws our defense back on the field when they were expecting to go out. Some teams will give you hard play-action and try to throw the ball down the field for the big play. We will also play MTF, which is the same thing, except we are in man with a free safety in the middle. The support on run for the linebackers will be about the same. Our huddle call is tight 7. That is a three-deep scheme. If they are a tight end-oriented team, we get our extra player to the tight end side. If they run the ball to the split end side, we get our safety that way. If they come out in an offset halfback, that would normally dictate where the safety would go.

The defense has to understand two schemes. The strong zone puts the strong safety to the strongside, and the weak zone puts the free safety into the split end. If we get the offset to the tight end, we call left. A *buzz call* from the strong safety means the extra man is supporting left. When we get the buzz call left, we get a *backer call right*. That means the primary support right is the Buck linebacker. Just before the ball is snapped, the Mike linebacker moves about a half a step to his right and stacks behind his nose tackle. The Buck linebacker slides into a stack position behind the 3 technique tackle. The strong safety is coming from his two-deep look, and on the snap of the ball, he ends up in a C-A alignment, which is the inside shoulder of the tight end at a depth of eight yards.

On the snap of the ball, the free safety goes to the middle third. The corners, for all intents and purposes, are playing loose man-to-man on the number 1 receivers to their sides. We like to press our corners and bail them out at the last moment into a very soft alignment. We tell our Mike linebacker to run through the inside heel of the fullback wherever he goes. If the fullback goes to the tight end side, the Mike linebacker fills the strongside B gap from the inside out. If the tight end blocks down, the Will linebacker spills everything to the strong safety up on the outside. If the tight end base-blocks or arc-blocks, the Will linebacker cuts him off and turns it up inside of him. The safety fills where he is needed. The Buck linebacker on flow away plays slowly for the cutback.

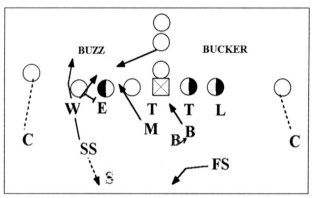

Zone the formation

If the ball goes to the split end side, the Mike linebacker has the weakside A gap. The Buck linebacker reads the flow and reacts accordingly. On tight flow, he is scraping outside.

If you are a split end-oriented team or you come out and give us an offset weak, we want the support player to the split end side. In our minds, we are going to play a weak three-deep zone. The offense comes out; the Mike linebacker makes a left call, because the tight end is left. The strong safety makes a backer left call, because he is going to the middle third. We are set in our gaps. The Mike linebacker aligns in the B gap. The Buck linebacker is in a head-up alignment on the weak tackle. The only thing we have left to do is make adjustments according to what the quarterback does before he snaps the ball. The quarterback offsets the back to the split end side. We get a *sky call right*. That brings the free safety up into the support position. The linebackers cheat back toward the strongside. The Buck linebacker becomes the inside-out player in the alley from his A gap alignment. The Mike linebacker moves into a stack position behind his end. If the play went to the weakside, the safety would be the unblocked player. If the play went to the strongside, the Mike linebacker is the unblocked player. The linebacker always cheats away from the support player. The first linebacker inside the support player is a fast-flow player. He runs inside out through any gap he can find. The strong safety is the middle-third player.

If the formation breaks and becomes a different formation, we have to find the break. The first thing we do is to find the tight end. He is left, so we make the left call. There is only one back in the backfield. The corners are playing the wideouts. They

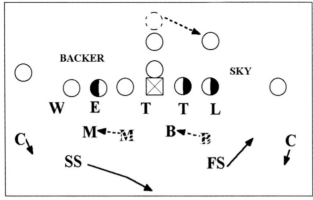

Zone the formation weak

have it easy. The broken back from the backfield is in the slot left. We call sky left. The free safety calls backer right. On any type of one-back gap run, our left linebacker has the B gap, and our right linebacker has the weakside A gap. The only exception to that rule would be a speed option of some kind. If they get that, they are fast-flow players. If the slot comes in motion to the split side, the safeties spin the coverage. The free safety calls sky right and becomes the support player that way. The strong safety becomes the middle player and calls backer left. Again, the key is not to let teams beat you up the middle running or throwing.

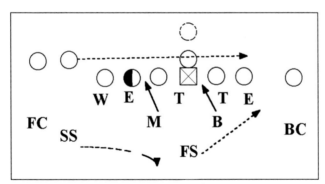

Zone the formation versus one back

If we played *man the formation*, it would be just like the zone, except the Will linebacker would have the tight end man-to-man. The gap responsibility is exactly the same. This might sound like a lot for a linebacker to learn, but it really isn't.

Let's go back to the slide front. When we played our slide front this year, it gave up something like 1.7 yards a carry. We are not an attack-front team. We are coming off the ball, but we are reading the front. We want to make sure nothing comes up the middle. With this defense, we normally are playing some form of two-deep coverage. If the offense has a good run balance, there is a good chance that we will be in cover 4. In a balanced running attack, we probably will need both safeties. If it is an "I don't know" down, we probably will be in cover 6, which gives us cloud support to the weakside and read support to the strongside. I don't like blitzes from this defense. If we blitz on this defense, we use the safeties as the blitzers. We key the uncovered linemen and ball on and off the line for support keys with our free safety to the split end side.

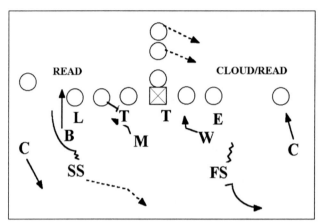

Slide defense—read or cloud

If a team has a tendency, play it. Remember to practice the exceptions to your defensive schemes. When linemen start to move their splits in and out, be aware of what they can run. If the splits are wide on the tight end side and tight on the split end side, it could be a counter strong. When the inside splits start to open up, that is trap or isolation. When the splits tighten up from the outside, you should expect to see sweep or some type of pass.

Gentlemen, it has been a pleasure. Thank you very much.

11

Linebacker Drills and Techniques

Don Pellum
University of Oregon
2002

I appreciate the opportunity to speak at this clinic and visit the state of Hawaii. I would like to congratulate the University of Hawaii on the season they just had. I had a chance to watch a couple of their games, and they really got after people. Congratulations to Kahuku High School for winning the state playoffs here.

I recruit the Los Angeles area, and I have also recruited Florida and Texas. One thing I know about the football here in the islands: No one plays with more intensity than they do here. That is a tribute to your kids and to the coaches who coach them. I love watching your kids play.

I came to the University of Oregon in 1992. I coached the linebackers in a 3-4 scheme and in a 4-3 scheme. I coached the defensive line for a year. That was the best thing I could have done for myself. It helped me understand how the linebacker fits with the defensive line in their responsibility. I coached the safeties for a year, and now I'm back with the linebackers.

I have one thing to say before I get started with my presentation. I am blessed to be on the staff at the University of Oregon. We have been together for a long time. Our defensive line coach does such a good job with his players. They get up the field and play really aggressively. However, they are so well coached when they feel pressure, they do a good job of staying in their gaps. We are not a great defense, but we are solid. We force people to do things they don't want to do if they plan on beating us. Our gap control is really solid, and as the year goes on, we get better at it.

My linebackers can read and they can run. I coach the crap out of them, and I never want them to slow down. I don't want to see a linebacker locked up on a block. We want to read and run. We are able to do that because the defensive line is so good in their gap control that they occupy a lot of attention. All the coaches on the defensive staff at Oregon do a great job of coaching their players. Put the talent level with the coaching and you can have a good defense.

Today I want to share some of my experience, our drill work, and the defensive scheme itself. I think a large part of the success we've had at the linebacker position is because of our drills.

In 1997 I had a sophomore linebacker, Peter Sirmon, who led the conference in tackles. In 1998 I had two guys in the top 20 in the conference in tackles. In 1999 I went to the defensive line, and in 2000 I had two guys in the top 12 in tackles. I am excited about that. I am not bragging, I am just telling you what our kids have accomplished. I think it is the system they play in that leads to their success. This year we had three guys in the top eight in the tackles in the PAC-10. In the top 18, we had five guys. In the top 10, we had three linebackers and a strong safety.

I want to force leadership on the linebackers. When the linebacker is calling the defensive signals, he is the leader in the defensive huddle. I am going to force our entire linebacker corps to lead everywhere. If you have a kid come to the University of Oregon, he is going to be kicking butt on the field, in the classroom, and everywhere. I hold them to high accountability on their role as leaders.

We have mentors with our young linebackers. We want to be a great group of linebackers. The veterans are in charge of the young guys. The young guys don't have to listen to the older players, but if they make a mistake, I'm coming down on them hard. If the veterans are not helping the younger players, I will be on them hard also. That is our system.

I have our entire group of linebackers over to my house for dinner. The seniors are in charge of all the duties at the dinner. They decide who peels a potato, who makes the Kool-Aid, who cleans up, and everything that goes on at the dinner. They are seniors and have earned that right.

When it comes to the football field, the best players play. If the senior is not the best guy, he can't expect to start. I encourage our guys to come in and do extra things to work on their skill level or increase their knowledge. During the off-season, we can't meet with our kids. But I can guarantee that twice a week my linebackers will come into the coaches' office on their own to watch film.

I want all the linebackers on the same page. When they come off the field, I want to be able to talk to them about what is happening on the field. I can't always tell what play is being run from the sideline. When I bring a linebacker off the field and ask him what happened, he can tell me. He can say, "Coach, that was a 24 power play. It didn't come outside; it broke off in the A gap." From there we can talk, and each of us knows what the other one is saying. If he tells me, "I saw the guard pull, and I missed the scrape, I really don't know what happened." Now I have got problems communicating because I don't think he understands what went on.

They don't have to come in. There are a bunch of random things they can do. If you don't know what to do at Oregon, you will never play. If the kid is on scholarship he has a right to be on the team. Playing is a privilege. If the linebacker wants to play and compete at this level, there are some extra things he is going to have to do. They are here to do two things. They are here to play football and go to school. The social issues will take care of themselves. If the young linebacker can't meet with the rest of the linebackers because he doesn't have time, he is not managing his time very well.

We run three fronts and I will talk to you specifically about one of them. What I would like to do now is go over our general alignments and reads in that front. Afterward I'll put on the drill tape and show you some of our drills. I brought some game tapes so you can see the scheme at work. At the end, if we have time, I'll put on our blitz tape.

Our base front is the *over front*, which we run about 75 percent of the time. We are a base 4-3 defense, which is overshifted toward the tight-end side. The Sam linebacker is aligned three to five yards outside the tight end and off the ball. His key comes from logical thinking. The person that can block the Sam linebacker first is the tight end. Therefore, the tight end becomes the Sam linebacker's key. He is keying the tight end to the near back. We never want to get more than a yard and a half deep in the backfield. If a sweep play comes toward the Sam linebacker, he wants to meet the blockers a yard-and-a-half deep behind where the tight end was aligned.

If the fullback is in the heavy set or strong halfback position, the Sam linebacker tightens his alignment to the line of scrimmage. When the blocker moves closer to the force point, the Sam linebacker has to do that also. If the set is a light set and the fullback is on the other side, the Sam linebacker can get more depth off the ball and get ready for the cutback.

We want to beat the fullback to the force spot, which is a yard-and-a-half behind the tight end. We don't want to get any deeper. If the Sam linebacker does, he will get kicked out, and everything gets inside of him. We want to force the play to bounce outside. We want to force the back to do something he doesn't want to do.

If the Sam linebacker sees the ball go inside with a full flow from the backfield, he starts to shuffle laterally. He does not want to capture the line of scrimmage. He wants to stay off the line of scrimmage about one-and-a-half yards and play the bootleg pass at him. If it is bootleg toward him, he has the tight end going to the flat. When he sees the full flow of the backs going away from him, he plays the bootleg by the quarterback.

If the tight end slams into the tackle and releases flat, the Sam linebacker won't see him unless he is off the line of scrimmage. If the Sam linebacker shuffles off the line, the tight end will run right into the linebacker. Now the Sam linebacker has a chance to cover him. If there is action totally away, the Sam linebacker becomes the fold and cutback player.

We play defense in the *battlefield*. The battlefield for us is two yards behind the line of scrimmage and three yards on our side of the line. We want to defeat blocks and attack everything that is in that area.

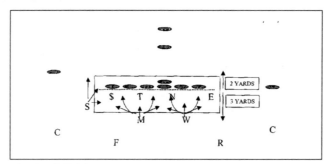

The battlefield

The Mike linebacker aligns in a 30- to 40-technique. He is four to five yards off the line of scrimmage. We want him deep. His alignment depends on the alignment of the fullback. The Mike linebacker is totally responsible for the A gap to his side. On any vertical play toward him, that is where he is going to attack. The Mike linebacker reads the nearest threat to block him. The offensive guard is the first threat to the Mike linebacker. The linemen are a consistent read for the linebackers. If the Mike linebacker sees the guard fan out on the 2-technique and both backs full flow to him, he attacks them as deep in the backfield as he can.

In our defense we always have what we call a *free hitter*. It is either the free safety or the rover. We play a lot of man-to-man coverage in the secondary. Sometimes both the free safety and rover are in the box.

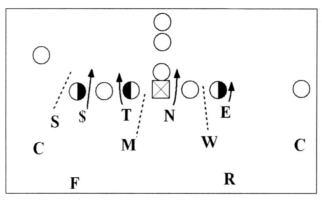

Base over defense

The Will linebacker is in a 20-alignment to the open side. Again that is depending on where the fullback aligns. He is reading through the guard to the backs. On flow toward him, he is filling the B gap. Our Will linebacker this year was a small kid. He was 5'10" and 210 pounds. You will see him in the film. I had trouble getting him to be patient. He was always getting too tight to the line of scrimmage and getting blocked. He was hell on wheels when he got moving.

With two backs in the backfield we will play quarter coverage, cover two, and a fair amount of man coverage. We disguise what we are doing, but you can expect to get a heavy dose of man coverage. We blitz a lot out of that set also.

I lost three seniors last year to graduation. The group that played this year really played well for us. They had never really played a lot before this year. We don't have any big-name guys playing on our defense. Our Sam linebacker is 6'1" and about 215. He was a corner but was so reckless the defensive secondary coach gave up on him. They didn't want him, so I took him. He has never run anything higher than a 4.45. The Mike linebacker is 6'1" and 235. He is the strongest linebacker I have ever had. He runs about 4.6 in the 40-yard sprint. The Will linebacker is 5'10" and 210. He is a tiny little guy who is all heart.

If the offense runs a power play to the tight-end side, they will pull the backside guard for the Mike linebacker. They double-team down with the tackle and guard on the 3-technique. The tight end blocks down on the 7-technique. The fullback is kicking out on the Sam linebacker with the backside guard pulling through the hole for the Mike linebacker. The center blocks back on the shade tackle.

The Mike linebacker is tracking on the fullback. He takes a lateral step when the double team comes down on the defensive tackle. He sees the fullback heading for the off-tackle hole. He has to beat the fullback to that point.

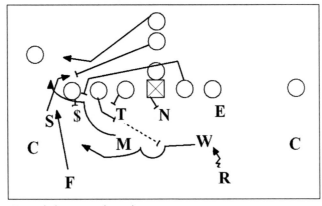

Over defense and reads

The Will linebacker sees the guard pull. The first thing he thinks is trap. He plays downhill right now and finds the back. If he sees the back coming inside, he has to take him. The guy to stop the trap is the guy that sees the pull. He is looking to get right off the butt of the tackle. He is playing over the top of the center's block on a trap. If it continues on, he scrapes outside.

When a linebacker is reading a play, he has to find out who is going to block him. If you want to make plays as a linebacker you have to know who is going to block you and beat the block. Playing linebacker is not like playing safety. On every play someone is trying to block you. Once you beat the block it is only a matter of running to the ball.

I felt like to beat those blocks, we had to get better using our hands. Before practice we go out and do a series of drills. Eight to 10 minutes before practice, we go out and do these drills. The linebackers do them on their own most of the time with the seniors in charge. I check on them from time to time to make sure they keep up their intensity and don't play too much.

I'll go through the drills and tell you what we are trying to do, and then I'll show you some drill tape so you can see them. In my drill, I try to fatigue them. There is never a long line in any of my drills. I want to condition as well as work on skills. I break them into two groups so I can get quick 10- to 15-second bursts, with one group going for 10 to 15 seconds, and the other group going for 10 to 15 seconds. I also want to give them a focus point. In the hands drill, there are two guys paired up working together. One of the drills is a hand-slap drill. The first player puts his hands up, and the other player will slap them down and do a swim move. Some of these drills are boring. To keep them focused, I'll tell them that today they are playing a team that only punch out with the hands, but they don't try to hold. In that drill, we only break the elbow down before we swim.

The next day I'll tell them we are playing a team that does a lot of holding when they block. In this drill, we have to slap the hands down, grab the elbow, and swim. That gives them a focus and breaks up the monotony of the drill.

I was at an NFL camp a couple of years ago watching practice. I was standing with a group of other coaches watching some drill work. I overheard a comment from one of the coaches. He said the drill they were doing was a worthless drill. I didn't say anything, but in the back of my mind I thought there is no drill that is really worthless. It is what you are trying to get out of the drill that is important. We don't know what the focus of the drill really is. We may be working on the hands in a drill, but the purpose of the drill is to gain footwork. If you are on the outside, you don't know what the focus of the drill is.

Most of the drills I do, you guys probably have done. We are big on fundamentals. The drill may look simple, but these are the drills we do. If you have an old speed-punching bag, I would put that sucker up and have everyone work on it. I would use it year-round. There is no substitute for a linebacker with quick hands. Linebackers are playing in a five-yard box, which is like a small tunnel against any offensive lineman. They are going against a lineman that knows where he is going and knows the play. He knows the snap count which gives them the advantage.

We want to give our kids some artillery to counter what they are doing. Part of that artillery is the drill work, and part of it is changing up the attack. Sometimes when we take on an isolation block, we take them high, and sometimes we cut them. We are going to take the fight to the blocker and slow him down.

The first thing on the tape is a sled drill. I found an old sled that the offensive linemen weren't using. I painted numbers on the sled dummies. I painted five numbers on the dummies. I painted one in each corner section of the dummy and one number in the middle. When the players are doing the drill I stand behind them. The first two days we did the drill, they didn't want to do it because they were tired and didn't want to stay in the ready position that long.

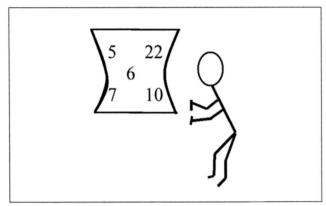

Sled drill

On the third or fourth day they were over the fatigue and started to concentrate on the numbers. I stood behind them and yelled out numbers. They have to hit the numbers with their hand as I yell them out. It makes them use both hands and focus on certain parts of the dummies.

The next drill is a partner drill. The players face one another, and they alternate back and forth. This is a pass-rush drill. I want them to be aware of where their hands are. The sled is stationary, but the partner drill is against a moving target. We start out with the progression of wrist, elbow, and shoulder. The first guy slaps the wrist down with his right hand on his partner's right wrist. He punches the right elbow of his partner in with his left hand. He finishes by punching the left shoulder with the right hand. As soon as one player does all three moves the other guy repeats the same three moves. He starts as soon as the other player's hand punches his shoulder. He starts by slapping the wrist of the hand that is on his left shoulder with his opposite hand. He punches the right elbow in with his left hand, and punches his partner's left shoulder with his right hand. They work back and forth on each other going as fast as they can. Once they become proficient in the wrist, elbow, and shoulder, we add a swim or club move.

In another hand-movement drill, we practice pass-rush escapes. I teach them the club-swim, club-rip, chop-club-swim, chop-club-rip, and double-arm up. I teach these moves to everyone, but they only use maybe one or two of these moves when they pass rush. Along with the hand movement I teach short quick steps. When a pass rusher overstrides, it is easy for him to get pushed off balance. Once they get past the blocker, they have to sink their hips and get their balance back. The pass rush is not over when the rusher beats the blocker; he has to finish the deal.

Another drill we do is the push-pull drill. This is a pass-rush move that does just what its name says. The move is to push back on the blocker and then pull forward and incorporate a swim or rip as you pull forward.

From individual drills, we go to group drills doing the same thing. We chop with the inside arm, club with the outside arm, and rip with the inside arm. In all these drills it is generally a three-step movement. We are trying to get to the back of the shoulder and pull it down.

At Oregon we don't play a lot of nickel defense. I have been blessed with linebackers that can cover in man coverage. That lets us keep them in the game in passing situations. Every day I do one of these drills out of this category. We do a trail technique, backpedal drive, and crossover techniques. I teach a couple reps of each move. The rest of the teaching is done in the 7-on-7 drill later in practice.

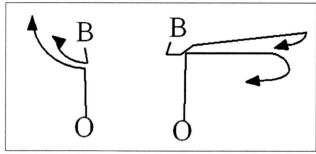

Trail drill

The next drill we do is called the *red ball drill*. I have these large red balls. I use this drill to teach linebackers to sink their hip so they can deliver a blow. The coach stands behind the red ball and pushes it toward the defender. He pushes it toward one side or the other of the defensive player. The defensive player has to shuffle to get in front of the ball and punch down on it with his hands. Every time they touch the ball, I want the weight on the inside foot, and the outside foot back. This also teaches the linebacker how to scrape. If the linebacker is scraping as a lineman tries to block him, it is important for the linebacker to get outside before he engages the block. If the lineman hits the linebacker before he gets outside, the lineman will grab him, and the linebacker will never make it outside.

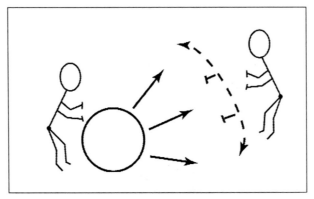

Red ball drill

When I do the red ball drill, I have half of the linebackers doing balls and half of them doing *hoops*. One group starts on the hoops and the other on the balls and they switch.

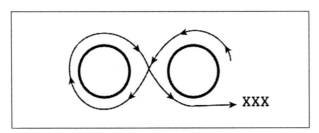

Hoops

I don't do a lot on the hoops, but I do make them run one-and-a-half laps just to make them work on their lean. Some of our guys are stiff and can't do this very well. I stand in the middle of the hoop and pull them around the hoop. They don't particularly like that.

Last year we lost games to Wisconsin and Oregon State. In those games we screwed up our fits with our linebackers. In the Wisconsin game, their running back had 32 carries for over 200 yards rushing. He had three carries for 182 yards. On all three of those carries, our fits were wrong. We had the safety and inside linebacker outside, and the running back hit it inside and took it to the house. We did the same thing in the Oregon State game. We screwed up our fits, and the run went to the house.

This year we had one play where we messed up our fits. That was against Arizona State. Other than that play, we were damn near 100 percent on our run fits.

Linebackers have to get across the tops of blocks to keep from being blocked. They have to get to the outside shoulder of the blocker, or he will pin the linebacker in a heartbeat. But I don't want the linebackers to be robots. We play really deep. The offensive linemen learn where we are and run up the field to cut us off. We can't have our linebackers fighting over blocks six and seven yards down the field. If the linemen get too high or too far up the field on their block, our linebackers run underneath the block.

We work drills to teach that skill. As part of the drill, we put him close to the line and have someone try to cut him. That makes him play the cut block off and get downhill to make the tackle.

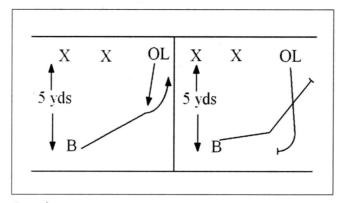

Over the top

We can add a second part to the drill by including a ballcarrier. The linebacker gets over the top of the offensive lineman and secures the tackle on the ballcarrier.

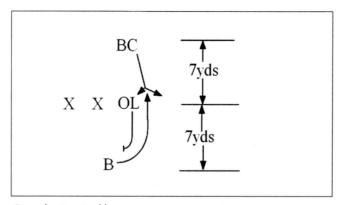

Over-the-top tackle

The next drill is the best drill I do. It is called the *fit drill*. It is a simple 1-on-1 drill. We have an offensive and defensive player. The defensive player is working to get his proper fit in the run game. The offensive blocker goes one way or the other. The defender has to get his proper fit and shuffle that way. We do this drill two or three times a week with two reps apiece. If the linebacker is an outside linebacker, he has to get to the outside of the blocker and shuffle that way. If he is an inside linebacker, he has to get to the inside and shuffle inside.

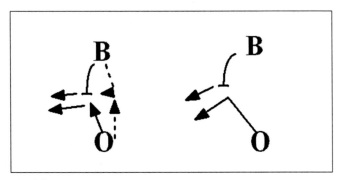

Fit drill

This next drill some of you might classify as a worthless drill. We line up our big pop-up dummies in a zigzag gauntlet-type alignment. Our guys run through the gauntlet clubbing the dummies with their outside arm. What this does is change the direction of their hips. Players are going to run in the direction their hips are pointing. Have you ever seen a pass rusher run right by the quarterback when he steps up? It happens because his hips are going in that direction and he can't turn back. This helps the linebackers to turn their hips and run downfield.

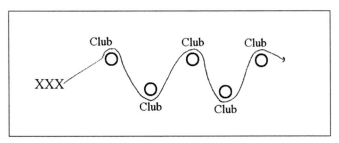

Gauntlet drill

The last thing on this tape is some sled work. I give the linebackers a shoulder that I want them to hit the sled with. We are hitting with the shoulder and getting over the top. The sled is an imaginary man. The linebacker hits the sled with his right shoulder; he has to move to his right to get to the next pad. In this drill we work on footwork and blow delivery. We are working on hitting the outside pad of a man. We want to defeat half a man, not the whole man. The problem with a sled that has five or six stations is you don't know who is hitting the sled and who isn't.

When we work on the one-man sled, we make them push it. You can tell who is hitting and pushing the sled. That is what I like about it. If you have seven people on a seven-man sled, you could have three out of the seven just hanging on to the sled and the other four pushing. On the one-man sled, there is never any question.

Our goal as a defense is to play fast. I want my guys to be unbelievably fast. I tell my guys if they go fast, they can't be wrong. Just don't slow down and get blocked. There are lots of plays in a game where the ball keeps bouncing outside. We want to dominate the game. We only get two opportunities to do that. We do not play offense. The only ways we can dominate the game is on defense and special teams. If you are a linebacker at Oregon and don't play on the special, you will never play in a game. You earn your way on the field as a linebacker by doing something big on the special teams.

There are a couple of things we need to do off the field to dominate on the field. You have to know your defense from all positions. Knowing your opponent is the second thing we need to do. That means we have to study. They get out of school at one o'clock. Our meetings start at 1:30. When I walk into my meeting room, the linebackers have been in there for 30 minutes watching film. If I understand my opponent and understand my defense, I can control the opponent. You cannot control something that you don't understand. We teach the big picture. If you are a linebacker at Oregon, you are going to take reps at all three positions. When we get on the field, we do our thing and play fast. When we are in the drills, we do all the base fundamentals together. When you understand what everybody else is doing, it makes it easier for you to do your job. The defense can go faster when they know what everyone else is doing.

When we play, we have to be the "baddest" dudes on the field. I tell them that and they have to believe it. For them to be successful, I need to give them a bunch of weapons. We are playing in that five-yard battlefield against guys that are bigger then we are. They are guys who know where they are going, know the snap count, and in our league, have a license to hold. We don't get mad about someone holding us because the referees don't call holding where we play. That is the way it is and we live with it.

If we are getting a lot of a certain play, we change up how we play the blocks. The Sam linebacker may tell the Mike linebacker that he is going to cut all the blockers on the counter gap instead of simply spilling the play. That tells the Mike linebacker the play is going to break really wide. We are going to change up and take the fight to the offense. We have to slow down the offense and gain an advantage.

If you want to go fast, knowing who is going to block you will help your play. Never get stuck on blocks. We want to read and run and beat the blocker to the force spot. It is ridiculous to think a guard can pull from the other side and block the linebacker in the hole. The linebacker should be in the hole waiting for the pulling guard.

We have to believe our eyes. When I played, I didn't have the confidence to move. I didn't want to screw up, so I played really slow until I understood that I needed to believe what I saw. When the guys come to the sideline, I want to know what they saw. If they can tell me, I don't get on them. For those guys who don't know what happened, they catch holy hell.

I've got three minutes left, and I'll try to show you four plays of our mix blitzes on film. We see a lot of option. Because of that, we have a read-out function. On certain blitzes, the linebacker determines who goes first. When people see our blitzes, there are a couple of ways to get outside of them. They screen and option to get outside on our blitzes. On these blitzes, we have one linebacker screaming through the line of scrimmage. The other linebacker moves laterally before he comes. If he sees anything that looks like a screen, he reads outside and gets into the play. That way we don't lose both linebackers on the blitz.

I did a better job of coaching that this year, and we were much better at the read-out function. We have a coverage control function also. That is so we don't lose both blitzes if a back swings in coverage. If the rover and Will linebacker are blitzing, in certain coverage they have to pick up a man if he releases. If the back releases and the rover back covers him, the Will linebacker keeps on coming on the blitz.

Quickly, I'll wrap it up. I appreciate the opportunity to share with you some of the things we are trying to do. The best thing we have going is a great environment and a bunch of good kids. We are really excited about our kids. I appreciate you getting up early and I really appreciate you guys not making me wear a shirt and tie. Once again thanks.

12

Big Plays by Outside Linebackers

Willy Robinson
Fresno State University
1990

I am the perimeter coordinator at Fresno State. That is just a title—a title to keep people happy type of thing. Basically, I coach the outside linebackers. That is the area that I have the most fun working with. I also coordinate the special teams. We deal with a lot of great talent. That is not the area that I am concerned with today. However, Ron Cox is a name that a lot of people in our area know about. He is a junior, but may go early in the draft. According to *Sports Illustrated*, he should be about the 14th pick in the draft. He had 26-plus sacks for us this year. That is as many as most people have in a career.

Today, I want to talk about getting our outside linebackers involved in our defense. We feel that big plays are made from the outside linebacker position. They are made by stunts coming off the perimeter. If you can get stunts from the perimeter and cone the offense, you do not have to have great athletes inside at the linebacker or down positions. You have people coming down from the corner making the area they have to defend inside a lot smaller.

Our dog *strong defense* is a mishmash of an eight-man front. This is what we start with in the spring. We have a reduction on the weakside and we are two deep in the secondary. The rover is a key man in this defense, and we vary his position on this alignment.

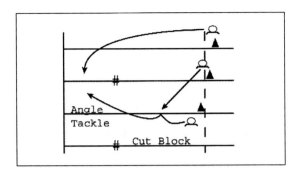

This may be the most important thing I say all day. We practice a great deal of the time on the get-off drill with the outside linebackers. It is a conditioning drill. We want them to get off on the snap of the football, but we will use something other than the snap count. We try to pick up some points through the scouting report that will give us a clue as to when the ball will be snapped. Let me go over some things we have picked up from films. In one case, the quarterback would come up to the line without his hands under the center. He would look around and check out the defense. Then he would put his hands under the center and the ball would be snapped immediately. We used this tip to work on our *get off*.

The next step on this came with the quarterback that would come up to the line and put his hands under the center, and then start scanning the field. Once his head stopped scanning, the ball was snapped. We used that as a get-off point. Our rover could see this better than the people down on the line of scrimmage. The people down inside must go on movement. We also used this type of quick get off with our inside linebackers on the blitz. We like to blitz. We blitz 95 percent of the time. We live or die by the blitz. Against the University of Utah, we ran the blitz 73 times out of 78 plays that they had the ball.

Our rover is the get-off man and I want him to be able to read the play by the second step. I want him to get read on the snap. The strike backer is the read man. He has to whip the tight end before he does anything else. We work out of a two-deep man or a two-deep zone. The strike backer is locked on that tight end. It allows inside linebackers to play more aggressive on play-action passes.

Against the split backs, we will still bring the rover off the corner, and make a combination call for the strike backer. If the tight end takes an inside release, the Mike backer is going to wall him inside. If the tight end continues his vertical stretch, the Mike backer is going to stay with him. If the tight end takes an outside release, the strike backer will straighten him up and run with the vertical stretch. If the tight end runs a flat route, we do what we call *swap it*, and the strike backer just sits in the curl area.

In the I back set, we run with the tight end on the vertical stretch. In the split backs set, we are dealing more with dropback passing situations, so we will combo off the tight end's release. The other set is the far back set. We can go to our 4-3 look just by making a backfield adjustment. Once we have the basics in our system, we work on a lot of schemes. We work with our players concentrating on keys.

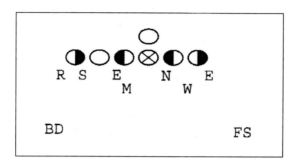

The first scheme we work on is the *fan*. It is a basic *dog kickout* play. The tight end fan blocks on the rover, who is coming off the corner. Our strike backer moves laterally with the tight end. When the tight end makes contact with the rover, the strike backer will skate back inside and maintain gap control.

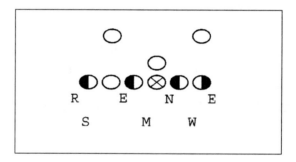

Our next scheme is against the power look. The tight end kicks out on the rover. The strike backer moves back to the inside. He has to realize the fullback is coming after him. The strike backer makes his first move laterally, then when he realizes the tackle is not on him, he knows that the fullback is coming at him. The thing that is important is that these kids have to know who is going to block them. They must know the possibilities.

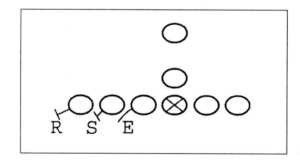

Next, we must face the counter. We are going to do something different versus the counter. We do not get many plays to the outside on this dog defense. We can take away a strongside run game.

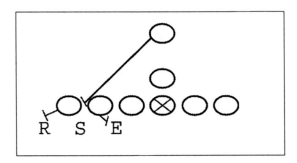

The strike moves laterally with the tight end, and then comes back to the inside. When he sees that the fullback is gone, the first thing he thinks about is the counter. We do something different on the pulling guard. Instead of the strike attacking the pulling guard with his flipper, he is going to move inside and close the hole. (The play is designed to go inside the pulling guard.)

Against the pass, we are still playing lock on the tight end. Now the tight end sets back in there to pass block. The strike still moves outside laterally, and now the tight end is gone, and he comes back inside and rushes upfield. He can come inside on a stunt of his own and rush the passer.

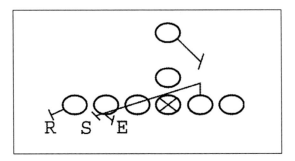

We give the strike a little freedom to play in this situation. These are some of the schemes we get out of our dog defense. We work on them every day.

Another scheme from the dog defense is the power. This is a scheme for the rover. For the most part, when we see this, we are talking about a slot formation where the two receivers are over on the other side. We give a *buzz* and a *saw* call.

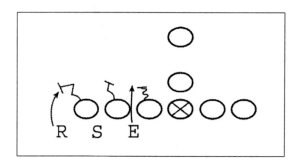

The *buzz* and *saw* comes from the defensive backer. *Buzz* is for the backer. If the safety calls "buzz," it tells the backer that he has contain. *Saw* is for safety. *Saw* tells the backer the safety has contain.

The other counter is a little different. All of a sudden, now we are getting kicked out by the guard. We are dealing with a slot situation here where we have our buzz and saw call.

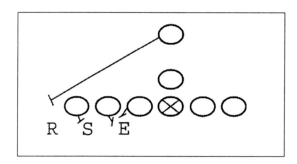

We always give aiming points. The aiming point for the rover versus I backs is the nose of the fullback. If that fullback goes away, he knows that his next read is the counter. We want to get off on the snap, and read the play by the second step. If we have a buzz or saw call on, the rover will come laterally down on the line and slip underneath the pulling guard and cut things off on the inside.

Our next look is from our 30 scheme. Here is a fan on the weakside pass rush scheme. Pass rush is knowing who and how they are going to block you. You have to be thinking about your pass rush move first. In this case, it is the tackle who is going to block the rover. The fan scheme is the first scheme we work on. We have the tackle block out. We have big-on-big. We have the guard on the end. He checks back to the inside linebacker, then he releases. He knows the first man he has to beat is our rover.

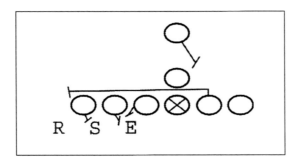

Our next scheme is our key pass rush. Here we have a base block. The guard checks the inside linebacker. He doesn't blitz, so the guard pulls out on the rover. The back checks, and then releases. Now we are dealing with a different man. If that is the case, we have a man that has to move more. It is more get-off and speed for the rover. We don't see a lot of this, because the rover is too quick in getting off. We do not see a lot of key protection.

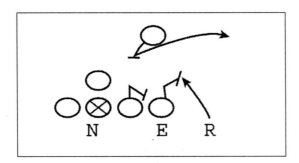

The next protection is the quick protection. The tackle base blocks down, and the guard blocks down, and the back tries to block the rover. We sell our kids on the fact that a back cannot block you.

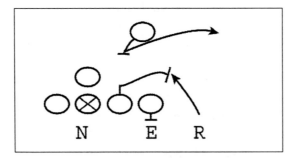

The other protection is the sprint draw away. They either pull the backside guard or the center. The rover, if he has contain rush, is going to work upfield, then come under the inside shoulder.

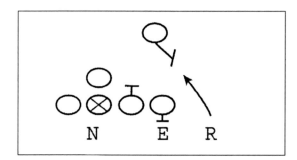

The bootleg pass protection is the same action as the spring draw pass rush scheme. The rover works upfield and comes underneath.

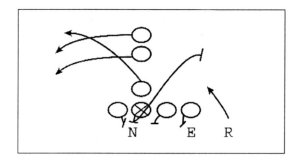

During our individual period, we work on get-off and our various pass rush schemes. This is without stunts and all of the other things. We do this every day.

We run a gauntlet drill that is set up in different areas of the field. The field is divided up. We have the receivers and the safeties in one area, the tight ends and down linemen in another. Everyone goes in the drill except the offensive linemen. We have the inside linebackers go against the fullbacks. Our outside linebackers go against the tailbacks.

This is how it works. We use a five-yard area out to the hash mark. We set cones up about five yards apart. The ballcarriers are lined up on the sideline. The tacklers are behind the cones. We get a lot of tackling done in a five-minute period. The ballcarrier sprints toward the cone. He gets to make one move. The tackler uses an arm-wrap tackle. We want the head across the bow, and we want good arm wrap. *We do not want any positive yardage by the running backs.* It is a contact drill in a limited spaced area, so you do not get many injuries. The cones are only five yards apart. Each defensive man gets three tackles. After each drill, the tackler moves up to the next cone and the first man goes back to the end of the line. You can get a lot of tackles in against quality offensive people.

The next drill we use is the run balance hit drill. We feel we need to work a lot on tackling. As much as we blitz, we get a lot of open field tackles. We use two sides of the field. We use a short side of the field from the hash mark to the sideline. You can teach your kids to use the sideline on this drill. We tell them to *use the sideline* on this part of the drill. We have three cones lined up on or near the hash mark. We use a ballcarrier, a cut blocker, and we have a tackler. On the command "hit," everyone starts running. This may not be a good drill for high schools, because you can't cut block. The blocker tries to cut the defensive man. The tackler comes off the block and uses the sideline, inside out, against the ballcarrier. We want a good high intensity tackle out of this.

On the other part of the drill, we add a blocker and use the other two-thirds of the field. Now, we use a reach blocker, a cut blocker, a ballcarrier, and a tackler. This is where we tell the kids to get off the ground and go. Get off on the whistle and go get the ballcarrier.

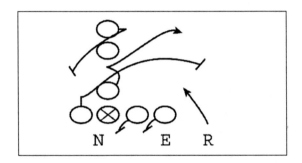

The reach blocker is in a three-point stance. He is like a tight end. The tackler is going to move laterally, using his hands, working upfield, staying square. His knees are bent, and he keeps his feet moving. This is an aggressive drill. The other landmark is the other hash mark. We do not do both drills in one day. We do the sideline drill one day, and the hash mark drill the next day.

The next drill is the best football drill that we have. We call it our *15-minute drill*. We start this drill on the very first day of spring drills. This is a drill that will tell you if the guys are in shape. This is a drill for all good football players. We can use the full length of the field, but, actually, all you need is 20 yards. The clock starts on the whistle. They start at the goal line.

Speed Form Run – They "form run" across the field. They go three-quarter speed. Once they cross the field, they turn and walk up to the next five-yard line marker. Next, they come back across the field at three-quarter speed on the form run. We look for good form and running techniques. We want them to run a straight line and we want them to pull that arm past their buttocks. We want them to stay focused during the entire run. We stress coaching points on the entire drill. They walk up to the next five-yard line and start back on the next line. They can walk down to the line they started out on, or they can move up to the next five-yard line.

Touch Run – Alternate Hands – They run across the field full speed, touching the ground with alternate hands. It is a full-speed touch run, alternating hands touching the ground. This drill really builds flexibility. After they get to the other side, they walk up to the next five-yard line. They go back to the other side with the same drill—touch run, alternating hands. Now they are back to the sideline where they started. They walk the five yards up to the next five-yard line.

Backpedal – Now they backpedal to the middle of the field. We want them to push off their toes. After they get to the middle of the field, they walk to the next five-yard marker, and then backpedal back to the sideline.

Backpedal Weave – They walk to the next five-yard marker and start the backpedal weave to the middle of the field. This is three-quarter speed. They get to the middle of the field and then walk to the next five-yard marker. They turn and backpedal weave back to the sideline. They should keep the shoulder near the ball down.

Backpedal Turn – Open Plant – They run the drill as a defensive back, and break back to the sideline.

M Drill – Three Plants – The M drill is where the player drops back five yards and plants his foot and comes forward to where he started. The second part of the M drill is for 10 yards. It is a little cha-cha step.

Turn Drop Drill – We work to the hash mark and return. We make two cuts.

Turn Drop Drill – Three Turns – We work to the middle of the field.

Spot Drop Drill – We want them to retreat, as they would on a pass drop. They can go four different ways if they turn the right way as they retreat.

Four Corner Drill – Now we use the goalpost. They backpedal 10 yards, and then carioca the width of the goalpost, then sprint to the goalpost, and then break it off. We come back and repeat the drill going the other way.

Quick-Feet Carioca – We have them go for 10 yards. We want the hips rotated 12 times, six in the first five yards, and six in the second five yards. They must do these fast to get them in.

Speed Carioca – Walk to the sideline and carioca the width of the field.

13

Linebacker Techniques and Drills

Jerry Sandusky
Penn State University
1999

Thank you. I want to start out by telling you a true story. We had a linebacker by the name of Jerry Gary. He was a great football player for us in addition to being a great student. He had a double major in engineering and business. He stayed on and did graduate work at Penn State as a graduate assistant. He worked with me with the linebackers. On game day, I was in the press box, and Jerry was on the sideline. We were playing Temple and weren't doing very well. I was upstairs telling Jerry what we should do, and Jerry was telling Coach Paterno. But as a typical head coach, he was not listening to any of my fantastic ideas. The game was going along, and I was getting frustrated. It finally got to be late in the third quarter, and we still weren't doing anything. Joe finally turned to Jerry Gary and told him to ask me what defense I wanted. I told Jerry to tell him that he has messed this game up for three quarters, so he could just foul it up the rest of the way. Jerry turned to Joe and told him I wanted this defense. He gave him the defense, it worked, and I was named defensive coordinator right after that.

Before I get into keys and play for the linebacker, there are some position coach recommendations I helped develop over the years that I want to share with you. These are basically for me, but this may reinforce some of the thoughts you might have. The first thing I mention is *being loyal to the other coaches*. We may argue, battle, and fight in meetings, but once we leave that meeting, we are going to have a positive relationship with our players and the other coaches. We learn to *work together as a group*, and that includes staff. We have to be *loyal to our players*. They are the only ones we have. They are not out there trying not to do well. You have to respect their efforts. Keep criticism in the meetings as constructive as possible. You have to *care about all the players*. I know that is idealistic. If we have done anything through the years at Penn State, this is the one we have worked on. The position coach has to be *enthusiastic*. He has to be *positive* and instill confidence in the players.

The next thing as a position coach is the most important and probably the most difficult thing to do. They have to *focus their attention on the most important details relative to their position*. Each one of us has a challenge. Each one of us has to get the players to perform as well as they can perform. You can't give them too much feedback, or you will have a confused player. However, if you are going to be successful, there has to be a certain amount of discipline, and they have to clearly understand what you expect of them. You have to analyze your position.

You need to *make the best use of the time available for meetings*. Meet as much as necessary, but not unnecessarily, to get the job done. Make sure the players understand what you are expecting of them. *Strive for perfection*. Make sure they execute the fundamentals and principles of their position properly. The last one is to *evaluate their performance, not their potential*. We have a saying at Penn State: You win with performance and lose with potential. There is always the danger of waiting on that player who looks the part. He runs well and is big and fast, but he doesn't perform. A lot of coaches get replaced waiting for those players to come around. It is not important how they look. It is important how they perform and execute.

You need to give your players constant feedback about how they are playing. I would like to think I do that, but I don't. It is important that each one of the linebackers I coach gets that feedback. You need to praise and reward good performances and encourage the players to play with a little imagination to make things happen. They can't be afraid to play recklessly. You need to organize every presentation you make and make it logical. Make a checklist of all the situations in which your players will be involved. You must understand the total defensive scheme.

There are some specifics we need to develop. The success that we have had at Penn State is due to the way we practice. We have developed a proper practice tempo. We have to work at full speed to develop the proper game-like habits. You must insist on second effort. There are no magic drills to make your people quicker. That comes from effort. You need to analyze your players in terms of what skills they need to develop. Determine what they need to improve on and how you can help them. You must evaluate yourself constantly. You have to understand the purpose of every drill you do. Devise or emphasize the special drills it takes to help develop each player. Make use of the simplest drill, because highly organized drills tend to waste time. Organize the drill to suit the number of players you are working with and the space available. Make sure all the equipment is on the field. There is nothing worse than trying to get the drill organized while everyone is standing around.

You have to analyze the teaching progression. Visiting Ohio State a long time ago probably did more for me in analyzing a teaching progression than anything I've ever done. You have to isolate the movements that it takes to get the job done. The drills must be done in segments. People need to be put into finish positions. Teaching tackling or blocking is done that way. After that, we go through the movements. We go over them versus air first. From there, you may go to one blocker. From there, it may be one blocker and a ballcarrier, but there is a progression to get to the finished product. When you are doing a drill, you want the players to be successful. You don't overwhelm them with everything first. Anytime you do a drill, do it full speed and correctly.

Organize and explain the drill and purpose off the field. Don't wait until you get to the drill to do that. Emphasize proper discipline, stance, and second effort. It is so easy to neglect that. But those will be the things that will beat you if you neglect them. Move the drills quickly. Don't dwell on any drill too long, and don't have too many people standing around not doing anything. We don't want boredom; we want movement and constant repetition. If the drill is not done correctly, it should be repeated. However, you can't sacrifice the entire group for one person. You want them to be successful. That may mean staying after or coming before practice until they are able to execute that. If they execute the drill correctly once, that may be enough. Instill as much competition in the drills as possible. Indicate the proper techniques, but don't overdemonstrate. As a coach, you want to get out there, do all the drills, and show them what to do. It is not important that the coach can do the drill. It is only important that the player can do it. Don't be afraid to be different.

When the ball is in play, everyone must be going full speed after it. That comes from discipline. Coaches have to concentrate on that. You can't have people standing around not going to the football. Players cannot play on the ground. You must emphasize that point. They must hustle and have second effort. Always work on your players' taking proper pursuit angles. You can come up with drills to teach these things, but the only way you can get it done is to insist on proper practice habits. Teach your players to play within the rules. That boils down to no penalties. You can go out, fight, bang heads, and do those types of things to prove toughness. But you will lose games if you don't have the discipline to play within the rules.

A defensive team must emphasize turnovers. All the things that you can think about need to be drilled. There are a lot of ways to turn the ball over. There are fumble recoveries, pass interceptions, blocking kicks, and all the reactions that go with the exchange of possession of the ball. Go over situations where you have to get the ball back. A sudden change, when your offense turns the ball over, is one of those situations. Your players need to have great game awareness. Don't forget to include surprise plays. Do not tolerate loafing, profanity, or anything that could be considered lack of discipline.

The next thing I am going to do is go through some of our fundamentals and principles of play and then get into our keys and recognition of plays. Our keys are not that complex, and I think it is important that you understand our fundamentals as they relate to what we are trying to get done with our defense.

The first fundamental is our stance. Our feet are approximately shoulders' width apart or slightly wider. Our toes are straight ahead. It is important that the weight of our body is on the balls of our feet. We bend our knees slightly and bend forward at the waist slightly. The only important thing about a stance is to be in a position where you can play off a blocker and make a tackle. You have to be in a balanced position to get that done. You have to be able to get underneath blockers and get to a pass zone. You have to be in that position when you are in the combat zone and people are ready to block you or when you are in the proximity of a ballcarrier. You have to be in a position to react and get something done. We emphasize being alert and tense from the waist down. A contracted muscle is going to react faster. In our upper body, we want to relax and appear confident. You want to give the impression that you want them to run at you.

We do things to emphasize stance. We do a quarter eagle drill, where we make a quarter turn on command. If I say right, they pivot, make a quarter turn to the right, and throw their shoulder that way. It is important that we do not hop or jump into the next position. We want to turn our bodies. The only thing we want to get out of this drill is the feel of a good hitting position. We give four commands, and after the last one, they sprint five yards. Every drill we do we want to finish with some kind of full-speed acceleration. Good football players can come out of the basic football position and attack people. We have them sprint and stop. That gives them the feel of being in that good hitting position.

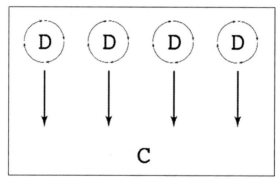

Quarter eagle

We are kind of old-fashioned in terms of things we do. Most linebacker play occurs in a lateral movement. We teach that. The first part of the drill is a slide or shuffle by the defender. We lean in the direction we are going, move the opposite foot, and kick out the foot closest to the direction we are going. You want them to go as fast as they can without hopping or jumping. If we don't have to cross our feet, we don't. The emphasis is on staying down in the good hitting position. We don't want to raise and lower our bodies. The last phase of this drill is the lateral run. We still feel that the best position to be in is with your shoulders square to the line. This drill is a stand-up wave drill. When I put them into the lateral run, I stop them to check whether they have raised or lowered their stance. The last thing they will do is the five-yard sprint out of the drill.

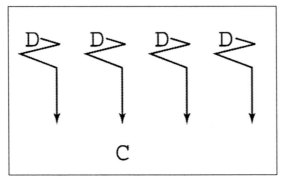

Slide drill, lateral run

The next thing we do is called a *mirror crossfield drill*. We have a ballcarrier and a defensive player about four yards apart. The defensive player stays slightly behind the ballcarrier. That position forces the ballcarrier to go east and west. The ballcarrier starts out and walks for about five yards. Then he will sprint full speed for about seven yards. At that time, he goes back to walking. He continues to do this until the point you have chosen by the use of a blocking dummy. When he gets to that point, he can cut back or go around the dummy. When the ballcarrier walks, the linebacker slides. When the ballcarrier sprints, the linebacker runs laterally. The linebacker stays square until the ballcarrier turns upfield. When that happens, the linebacker attacks the ballcarrier. If the ballcarrier went around the bag, the defensive player would execute a tackle on him.

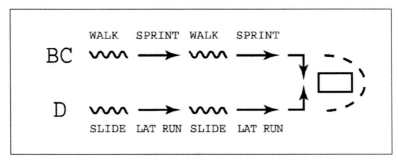

Mirror crossfield

The next drill is a simple around-the-bag drill. We put a dummy down on the ground. We put a leader on one side of the dummy and the defender on the other side. The point is to emphasize two things. First, we don't want to get overextended.

Good football players don't get into a position where their heads and shoulders are too far out in front of their feet. If they do, they will probably fall down. Second, we want to make our second move first. Making contact is not good enough. We have to make our second move first. The leader starts the drill by coming to one side of the dummy. The defender moves the same way and moves into the leader. He accelerates his feet and moves into the leader. After that, it becomes a race to see who can get to the other side of the dummy. The defender has to recover from the push and get to the other side. They do this four times. On the fourth time, the defender takes the leader back five yards in a run-through tackle.

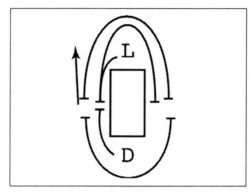

Around the bag

An additional movement drill is a mirror score drill. We have two bags on the ground about seven yards apart. The leader would be positioned at the top of the bags, and the defender would be right on him. To start with, we may have the defender put his hands behind his back to emphasize that this is a foot-movement drill. We don't want people reaching with their hands. The leader is going to use finesse to fake out the defender and get across the line five yards away between the two bags. When we do this drill for real, the defender can use his hands and anything else to keep him from getting across the line. The defender slides and jams, but he can't get overextended. We run the drill for 10 to 15 seconds or until the leader scores. If he scores, he goes back to the beginning and tries to do it again.

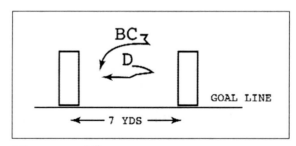

Mirror score drill

This is the box drill. It is a rectangle about 25 yards long and 18 yards wide. We have a ballcarrier whose sole purpose is to stay free within the confines of that box. The other player in the box is a blocker. He is trying to protect the ballcarrier. The defender is trying to get to the ballcarrier. The ballcarrier has to utilize his blocker and stay clear of the defensive man. The defensive man uses pass rush techniques to get to the ballcarrier. We do the drill for 15 seconds. If after about seven or eight seconds the defensive man has not gotten to the ballcarrier, we would call the blocker out. Now the ballcarrier is on his own, and the defensive player must get him before the 15 seconds are up. We do this drill in our indoor program.

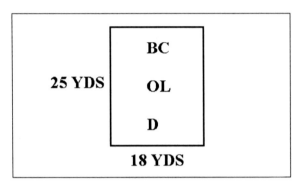

Box drill

The next area is playing off blocks. This is becoming more and more difficult with the increased holding that takes place. There are some basic principles that we would still emphasize. The first one is to concentrate on the blocker first, regardless of the defensive scheme. You have to see the ballcarrier out of the corner of your eye. If a blocker comes at us on an angle, he is trying to get position on us. We use our hands to protect ourselves. In our situation, that blocker could come below the waist. When the blocker moves his head to one side or the other, now we have to get even with the blocker. He is going to try to cut me off and get position on me. If he comes below the waist, I have to stop his charge. I push with my hands. I am going to slide, push with my hands, and get my feet clear of his charge. The point of emphasis is that I have to make my second move first. I have to be the first one to move after contact. When I clear my feet, I want to get my outside foot back. I have never seen a good linebacker playing with his outside foot forward with the ball to the inside.

If we are playing on the line of scrimmage, we use our hands all the time. We get under them, butt them, and explode the hands. I have to do something to neutralize his charge. That is the punch. Now it becomes a fight to get the offensive blocker's hands off the defender. There is no answer to the holding. We practically use martial arts to get their hands off us.

If we are off the line of scrimmage and the blocker comes straight at us, we will use the shoulder and forearm into him along with the opposite hand. We don't take a side with the blocker coming straight at us. We take a short jab step with the foot to the side of our shoulder and forearm. We drive our arm out from the body, bending the lower arm slightly. We stay square and get underneath the blocker. The opposite hand comes up to try to get some sort of control of the blocker. From that position, I strain out and into the pressure and up through the pressure of the blocker. But we can't get overextended. I should have said this first. If the linebacker is quick enough to make the tackle without taking on all these blocks, he should do it. The object is to make tackles. We have had linebackers so obsessed with killing blockers that ballcarriers would run right by them. I've had players so good and quick that they didn't get hooked up with blockers. The worst part about using a forearm in this technique is that the offensive players just grab and hook the forearm, but we have to fight off laterally to get into position to make the play.

Anytime a defensive player is in a shade technique, he will have someone coming down on him at an angle. We want to play as square as we can. I am going to try to change his angle with my athleticism. Most of the time, the defensive player is a better athlete than the guy who is blocking him. I am going to make him think by anticipating the types of plays that he is coming down on me. The point of emphasis is to stay square with the shoulders. We never want to run around the block, but we may take a chance and try to beat the blocker underneath.

The teaching progression would start with playing on air. They get in their stance. I give them a direction; they slide and butt the blocker. We want to keep the elbows in and punch the blocker. As far as the forearm technique, we use the hit-hit-hit drill. We slide and simulate giving the forearm. We keep the elbow in and everything in a straight line without wasting any motion. We don't want them to wind up when they throw the forearm. We would hit and hit again, and on the third hit, we strain and push off. From there, we would go to the slide, push, and give, as if we were playing off a chop block. The emphasis would be on keeping the shoulder square and dropping the outside foot. We practice that on air.

The next part would be to use a machine sled. We get into the fit, accelerate the feet, strain, and get off the block. We hit, hit, hit in this drill also. The next thing is to have someone with a shield coming down as the angle block from the outside. We would execute our technique and get across the block. After that, we do the drills live. We use the one-on-one type of drills. During this drill, we have the offensive blocker try to grab the defensive player.

The next thing is tackling. We approach this drill with a good balanced stance, just like playing blocks. As the tackler approaches the ballcarrier, his head and eyes are up. The neck is bulled. We cannot control where the contact is going to be made, but upon contact, my neck is bulled, and I immediately raise my head. I don't want to get hurt, and if my head is down, I will go down. The feet are accelerated through the ballcarrier on contact. The player who wins is the one who does that. Don't waste motion by winding up the hands. Don't lead with the hands. That causes missed tackles. The hands come in the area of the rear end and slide up to the armpits.

When we tackle on an angle, our technique is very similar. When contact is made from the side, the tackler wants to turn his head and look at the ballcarrier, square up, and take him back. The head goes in front, but we want to work to square. In an open-field tackle, we tell them good luck. There are very few instances that are nothing but athleticism. I am very cautious about practicing open-field tackling. If you practice it too much, it becomes a mental thing. The only thing we tell them about an open-field tackle is know where your help is. If you are going to miss him, force him back to the help. We want to be the aggressor. We don't want to get out there and break down. We go after him. You have to gather yourself, but don't come to a stop and let him turn you around.

The last thing is on the goal line. Ballcarriers have a tendency to get airborne and jump over the line. If he tries to spring over the line, we spring from our stance and try to meet him in midair. The perfect example was Herschel Walker. We played them in the bowl game. We practiced for a month on meeting him in midair on the goal line. Sure enough, that situation occurred. We jumped and he didn't, and he ran right through the goalposts. That was a great job of coaching.

To drill this, we start out with a fit drill. We put the tackler in the position we want him to end in. We don't put the hands in until we are in a perfect fit, and then the hands come in. We accelerate the feet and take the ballcarrier back. We put a mat on the ground and a tube dummy in front of it. From the fit position, we take the ballcarrier back and into the mat. The mat is for the protection of the ballcarrier. After that, we put the ballcarrier on the edge of the dummy. The linebacker will be five yards back. On the ballcarrier's movement, the linebacker comes forward, executes the tackle, accelerates his feet, brings his hands, and puts him in the mat. We do it straight forward and at angles.

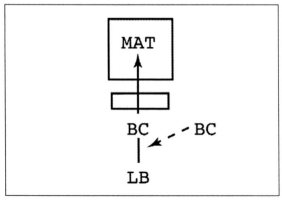

Mat tackling

The next drill is around a tube dummy. The ballcarrier is on one end of the dummies and the tackler is on the other end. The ballcarrier chooses a side. The tackler takes a lateral step and makes the tackle.

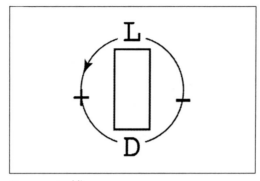

Dummy tackling

The next drill is a score drill. We set up five dummies on the ground. The ballcarrier is on one side of them, and the tackler is on the other. The ballcarrier moves from one side to the other, and the tackler mirrors him. Once the ballcarrier turns up in the alley, the tackler gets into the alley and makes the tackle.

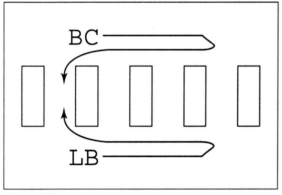

Score drill

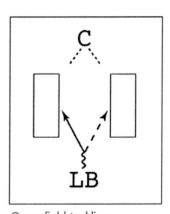

Open-field tackling

We use two bags to practice open-field tackling. The coach stands between the dummies, five yards from them. The linebacker flies up from the other side. The coach gives a direction, and the linebacker tackles the dummy.

Maybe once a year we would practice goal line tackling. We would use a bag. We would throw the bag over the goal line and have the linebacker meet it in midair. That would be a simulation drill.

There are combination drills we do that touch on some of the keys we have. We do a dive drill. We start out with a blocker and then add a ballcarrier. We do the drill on boards to start with. The offensive and defensive men are both on the board. That gives them the feel of not getting turned and getting under the blocker.

I like the 2-on-1 drill better. I have one linebacker and two blockers with one back. Both blockers are coming off straight. The linebacker is aligned on the middle bag opposite the back. The back chooses one way or the other. The linebacker scrapes, defeats the block, and makes the tackle.

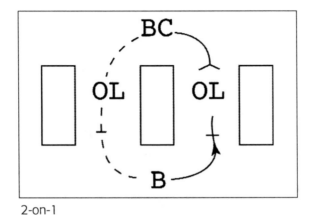

2-on-1

The third drill puts two linebackers in the drill. The back moves outside between the two dummies. The linebacker to that side will get a down block from one of the two blockers. He fights over the top and makes the tackle. The other linebacker works against a cutoff block. As he pursues, he gives ground, because that is his angle. If the ball is exposed when he gets there, he goes for the strip. They are working on inside tackling and not overrunning the ball.

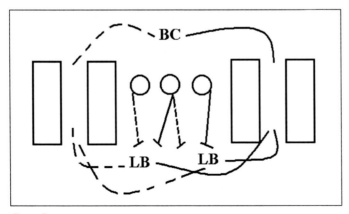

3-on-2

We do a 3-on-1 key drill. We have a ballcarrier, three blockers, and one linebacker. The outside blockers are coming down on the linebacker. The middle blocker is going to low-block him. The back takes the ball outside the outside blocker on each situation. The blocker watches the coach to see which one of them is going. The back breaks toward the block.

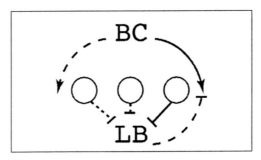

3-on-1

The next drill is a 3-on-1 drill also. This is called *blood drill*. It is a toughness drill. It is for quickness and explosion. I stand behind the linebacker and point to whomever I want to come. They deliver a lick on the linebacker and try to knock him back. The linebacker recovers and gets back into position. I point to the next guy. He does the same thing. When I raise my hands up and point, the lineman fires on the linebacker, and the ballcarrier runs with the ball outside the outside man. The linebacker delivers the punch, gets off the block, and makes a tackle.

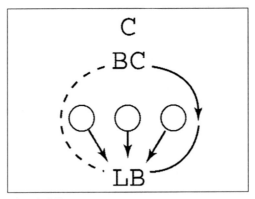

Blood drill

Let me cover pass coverage really quickly before I go to something else. From our initial stance, we have to get started well to get into coverage. When he sees pass, he turns and runs laterally back to his pass zone. His focus is back on the quarterback so he can recognize draw and screen. As he goes back, he glances for anyone threatening his zone. We want to play from inside to outside. We want to take away the closest throw. We want to position ourselves so we can do that. When the quarterback is ready to throw the football, the linebacker comes under control. He tries to position himself about three yards inside and three yards in front of a receiver in his zone. We match up with people. If the quarterback turns outside, he sprints, and at the last minute, he reaches out with his hands. He wants to put the ball away if he intercepts it and head full speed for the other goal. We don't want to turn the ball back over to them.

When we drill this, we work with the depth that they are going to see in the games. We start out at the finish position and break in and out on balls. Then we put him into his drop with a stationary receiver and do the same thing. The last thing we do is let the receivers run their patterns and let him make his drops. You might want to make up a drill where the ball is dropped off to a flaring back to teach the angle to the ball that you want taken.

If we play a man coverage, we want to be the aggressor. I don't wait for the back to come to me. I go in on him and attack his inside shoulder. I play a bump-and-run position on him. If we are playing an up receiver on the line of scrimmage, he has to know where his help is. If my help is outside, I can't let the receiver have an inside release. If he tries to release inside, the linebacker tries to push him down the line of scrimmage. If he makes the inside release, the linebacker has to get underneath and chase him.

If he takes an outside release, he can't overreact to that move. The receivers are good at faking the outside up move and coming underneath inside when you react. They used to tell you not to move until the receiver got past your shoulder, but the quarterbacks have gotten so good that they throw the ball right now on no movement to the outside. As he goes by me, I jam him with my outside hand, but I am really alert for the inside move. If he starts inside, the linebacker jams him hard with his inside hand and fights the release to the inside. If he goes by the linebacker, he gets on his inside hip and chases him, staying as close as possible.

We key what we call the *near triangle* with our linebackers. That means we look at the ball, through the uncovered lineman, to the back. If we are playing man-to-man coverage, we may just focus on the back. We would like to read the ball and flow all the time, but if we get a pull by the guard, that takes precedence over flow. The linemen will always tell us where that play is going. We have to be able to see the whole picture. Definite action is both backs going the same direction. Generally, you are going to get scoop blocking with that. That is basically what we would teach our linebacker, and we would try to apply that to various situations.

The other thing we would emphasize is some sort of isolation block. As a general rule, anytime a lineman turns out, you are going to get an isolation play. We want to attack the blocker on his side of the line of scrimmage if we can. The way we attack the blocker would depend on the defense we are in.

Thank you very much.

14

Linebacker Techniques and Drills

Bob Simmons
University of Notre Dame
2003

Let me say it is indeed a pleasure to be invited to the Coach of the Year Clinic by Nike and Earl Browning. I got a chance to know Earl when I was Oklahoma State. They were a Nike school and I spoke for him in a little different of a place than Louisville. I spoke at the Hawaii Clinic. The weather is just a little different over there.

Hopefully I can share some of the things that I believe in as it relates to *linebacker play*. I am proud to be a part of the Notre Dame staff. We have a great head coach. Tyrone Willingham not only has impeccable credentials, but also is a great person to work with. It was his vision that enabled Notre Dame to get back on track.

Growing up in Ohio, I always wanted the opportunity to coach at Notre Dame. When Coach Tyrone Willingham called to offer me the job, it was a no-brainer. If you know anything about Notre Dame, from the Golden Dome to Touchdown Jesus, it is a special place to coach.

I want to share a story with you. The Touchdown Jesus statue is on the face of the library. When I came to Notre Dame to visit and tour the campus, I was in the library and had taken the elevator and was going to the 12th floor. I wanted to see the mystique of Notre Dame and on the 12th floor there was a special priest who was world renown. He had counseled Presidents from all over the world. As we approached the 12th floor, the elevator made a grinding sound and stopped.

I was stuck on the elevator. I began to call for help. I called out, "Help, I'm stuck on the elevator." At that moment I heard a voice say, "No you're not." I thought it was divine intervention. As I heard the voice, I looked up and turned around to see a guy getting on the elevator from behind me. He said, "You're not stuck, this is the way out." That just goes to show you, when God closes one door, another one opens behind you.

I believe a linebacker has to be coached just like a quarterback. There are some *special characteristics* that go with a linebacker. The first thing we do as coaches is go right to the drill and technique work. I have learned over the years that before you can teach techniques and drill, you have to ingrain *leadership* at that position. All positions are important, but the linebacker is critical on defense. Everything that goes on within the defense goes through that individual. Everything the coordinator sends into the game comes out of the linebacker's mouth.

Everything he says affects the entire defense. When I first got to Notre Dame, I sat down with my linebackers and asked them why they wanted to play linebacker. There are qualities that the linebacker coach and coordinator expect the linebackers to have to play that position. We expect the linebacker to be the *heart of the defense*. Playing linebacker is a privilege and with any privilege comes responsibility. He has to understand the privilege he has been given and be ready to fulfill its responsibilities.

Leadership is the first and most important quality you look for in a linebacker. Leadership is influence. John Maxwell said, "People catch our attitudes just like they catch our colds; by getting close to us. One of the most gripping thoughts to enter my mind centered on your influence as a leader. It is important that you possess a great attitude, not only for your own success, but also for the benefit of others." The linebacker has to have the right *attitude*. I spend a lot of time with our kids giving them things so they understand the importance of leadership in the position of linebacker.

Clarence B. Randall was quoted as saying, "The leader must know, must know he knows, and must be capable to make it abundantly clear to those about him that he knows." The linebacker has to *increase his knowledge of the game*. He has to study film. He has to call the right defense. The players in the huddle have to believe that the linebacker knows what he is saying. In the huddle, the linebacker has to be in charge at all times.

Leroy Eims stated, "A leader is one who sees more than others see; who sees farther than others see, and who sees before others do." The linebacker has to recognize blocking schemes, formations, and be aware of what is going on around him. He has to anticipate things and give that knowledge to the group.

As coaches, we have to let the young men trying to play linebacker know what we expect from them. Your signal caller in the huddle must be your defensive leader. Never let this be questioned. He has to look into the eyes of every man in the defensive huddle and make sure they are looking at him. He has to have *discipline* in the huddle. He has to be sure that every man has heard and understood the call correctly. He breaks the huddle sharply. He always looks up and never makes a bad call in his own mind.

I had two linebackers this year who called the signals. One of them was clearly established as the leader in the eyes of his teammates. He got hurt and the other linebacker had to make the calls. He was not seen by his teammates as being the natural leader. Consequently, when he got in the huddle to make the call, it appeared as no one was listening to him. It was because of his presence in the huddle. He had not learned to have control and huddle discipline. He had to develop the attitude and charisma to get in the huddle, call the defense, and break the huddle without offending the player next to him.

The linebacker has to *execute the defense the best.* You cannot be a linebacker and not be the best. We expect the linebacker to know the defense position by position. He has to know what everyone on the defensive front is supposed to do in a particular defense. If one of your teammates lines up incorrectly, the linebacker should recognize this immediately and move him into position. If the defense is breaking down through an error of a teammate, he should be able to explain the error. In order to do this, he will have to study football.

In football we always talk about *effective communication*. Here is a saying that I've picked up that illustrates that idea. I pass this along to my coaches and players. It is called the *miracle of dialog:* "Every man is a potential adversary, even the ones he loves. Only through dialog are we saved from this hate toward one another. There is only one qualification for this dialog. It must be mutually perceived by the parties and pursued relentlessly." I know I'm talking about the position of linebacker, but I'm also talking about what happens between a coach and another coach or a husband to his wife.

When a linebacker is in the heat of the game and has to adjust the position of one of his defensive lineman or another linebacker, he has to use a *command* that reflects his leadership. If he gets emotional and curses at one of his teammates or coaches, oftentimes that person will get offended by it. If the linebacker says the right thing, players will follow direction and coaches will listen to you. I have seen players at the wrong time of a ball game stop communicating with one another. The wrong time is when the offense is driving on the defense. That is the time when communication has to be the clearest.

When you look at your films and find players out of position, the general excuse for the misalignment is, "I didn't hear the linebacker make the call." The reason he didn't hear the call was the way the linebacker said it. I happen to believe the way players talk to one another on the field is important. I believe when you are coaching a position, you need to take time to cover these communications. I do it in the spring when I have more time.

The linebackers should always *know and be aware of the down-and- distance*. The down-and-distance will predict every defense we call. The linebackers need to know what to expect on each down-and-distance situation according to the position.

He needs to be aware of the *field position*. This is equally or even more important than down-and-distance. You should know what the opponent will do when he is backed up to his own goal line. We have to know when he is likely to gamble on offense. We want to know at what position on the field they will go into their regular offense. When is the offense likely to use trick plays and when will they gamble on fourth down?

The linebacker has to know *how much time is left in each quarter*. Many games have been lost because a team misjudged the time left to play in each half and what an opponent can do during this time. In games where two teams are equal, the time employed intelligently by a team often determines the winner. The linebacker should know the number of time-outs his opponents has left, as well as how many time-outs he has left. Proper use of time-outs will win games for you.

Linebackers are not born with that kind of knowledge. The coach has to give him the tools and teach him to think. If you have a smart player playing for you and you want him to reflect your coaching, you better give him the tools to do his job. You have to give him those leadership qualities that you want. You are the coach and you have the knowledge and wisdom to pass on to these players. If you give them the wisdom and guidance, it is easier when the situation arises to talk about those things.

The linebacker needs to know the *tendencies and formations that the opponent is going to use*. We need to know if the offense runs away from the formation or runs to the formation. In addition to knowing the formation, he has to know the favorite play run from each formation. If we know his favorite play, we can force him to run something else to try to win the game. The linebacker has to make sure he adjusts the defense correctly to the formation. Formation tendencies and checks to those tendencies are the responsibility of the linebackers.

I have not had the opportunity to coach pro football, but I've been to several camps to observe. The one thing that impresses me about a pro defense is the amount of communication that is going on among the defensive players. When we get back on campus that is the one thing we wish our players would adopt. The reason they do it is because the coaches practice it, coach it, and give it to them. When the defense is communicating, we are really good. When we don't get that communication, we are not nearly as good. We are just not consistent at talking as a team.

The alignment of the linebacker is based off his *gap responsibility*. We have to spend time talking and practicing different techniques and alignments. The linebacker will be aligned in a one shade, a 2I, a 20, 30, 40, 50, and a 70 technique. They have to know where to align and which gaps go with those alignments.

The way I teach is called the *whole-part-whole system*. I teach the whole concept of the defense and then go back and break the defense down into its parts and the techniques that go with each part. When I do drills, I believe it is important for the players to know why you are doing particular drills. I do drills that are direct carryovers to the linebacker's responsibility as it relates to the defense.

These drills are used to teach and learn the basic fundamental skills of linebacker play. When we begin to do our drills, the basic drills are divided into several areas. We teach in a *progression of drills* that relate to the specific techniques of linebacker play. We teach movement drill. There are warm-up drills that we do before practice. Bag drills are used daily to improve foot movement and agility. We tackle daily in some type of tackling drill. We teach sideline tackling, circle tackling, and other forms. We teach proper position starting with a fit position, to a hit position, and finally to an approach and complete tackle. We systematically teach block-protection drills, which covers the rip and cut block. Finally we teach key drills, which feature stance, alignment, and key.

I'm going to show these drills on film and I'll go back and forth with their description and use them as I go through them. We don't use all the drills every day. Depending on the time of year and the opponent we are playing, the drills will be selected and adjusted.

There are certain things you must keep in mind and practice to improve yourself as a linebacker and a football player. Repetition is important to improve your skills, but you must avoid boredom in the drills. When you are doing drills, you have to pay attention to the little details. If players want to improve their skills they must work hard on the little things.

Your players have to *help each other improve*. They need to encourage each other in drills when things are done well and help each other to correct mistakes when they are made. If the players practice drills at full speed, they will learn to play at full speed. Each drill starts with an offensive movement and ends on the whistle. The player has to go all out from movement to the whistle.

Time is precious and time can't be wasted getting into position to run the drill. If a player doesn't know why we are doing the drill, how to do the drill, or how to correct of a mistake, he should ask. We want the linebackers to be competitive in a game-like situation so it helps them to become better. The harder the player goes in a drill, the better he makes himself and his teammates. It is always good for the player to know the tempo of the drill. He has to understand the difference between a teaching drill, thud drill, tag-offense drill, and scrimmage.

We have a *fundamental teaching progression* that we use in teaching stance, start, and keys. We are in a two-point, balanced stance. Having a balanced stance is the best position to start laterally without rising up, dipping down, or false stepping.

In our starts, we want to be able to start forward without giving away our stunts. In the lateral start we have to move the away foot first. We want to be able to lean in the direction of the key and start laterally by sliding or crossing over without false stepping.

There are a number of things we key. The linebacker keys the near backs inside shoulder. The linebacker keys the heads of the offensive lineman they are over. They have to key men in man-to-man coverage. If we are running a stunt, the linebacker knows where he is going regardless of the flow. He keys the ball to get a good takeoff and keys the linemen on the run. In the pre-snap read, the linebacker keys lineman or backs for tips by their eyes, stance, or alignment.

We use a number of different techniques in *shedding blocks*. We use position techniques first. On an aggressive high block, the linebacker uses his position technique getting his shoulder pads under the pads of the blocker. On the low block, the linebacker uses his hands to keep the blockers off his feet. Against a pass blocker the linebacker wants to use his hands and not get involved with the body. If the linebacker gets blocked he has to use a rocker step, give ground, and go. When he is facing a trap block, the linebacker uses lateral body reaction, stays square, and if caught he uses the rocker step and gets off the block.

When we teach *tackling*, we are looking at the man and want to run over him. At the moment of contact, the linebacker explodes, accelerates his feet, squeezes as tight as possible, and takes him back. When he gets into the squeeze part of tackle he wants to wrap up his arms and grab cloth.

We start our practice with what I call *movement drills*. They are general agility drills that are worked over dummies or bags. We don't do the same drills every day. We change them up to prevent boredom from setting in. This gets our blood flowing but we are practicing linebacker skills. We do a lateral run to start with. It is important for the linebacker to explode for five yards after he crosses the last bag. They start in a good football position with their shoulders down. They shuffle over the dummies, keeping their shoulders down and in a good football position. I watch their foot work as they go through the bags. I want the linebackers to move their feet. I don't want both feet down in the same hole. As one foot hits the ground the other foot should be up. I don't want both feet on the ground at any time. When one foot leaves the ground the other should be on the ground, and when one foot comes down the other foot should be off the ground. When we change direction later on in the drill, the linebacker will have a short step in between the bags. We work on not crossing over with their feet. We want them sliding and not crossing their feet. We want their eyes up feeling the bags and their hips as square as possible. In this drill we do the lateral run, buzz feet, lateral run, change direction, and forward-backward change direction.

If you want to add something to the drill, use your managers to flip balls to them as they go down the bags. They catch the ball and flip it back to the manager. You can

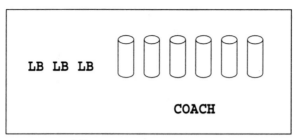

Movement drills

use two or three managers to do this. At the end of the dummies you can roll out a ball and have them scoop it up and score or recover it. You can have them angle tackle at the end of this drill. These drills relate to things that are going to happen in a game.

We use a drill called *shuffle-run-shuffle* that teaches the linebacker the techniques in pursuing a ballcarrier. We set up four cones. The first two cones are five yards apart with ten yards between the next two cones. They are five yards apart, just like the first two cones. The linebacker shuffles between the first two cones. He turns and sprints between the next two cones. As he reaches the second set of cones he has to square his hips and shoulders and go into a shuffle. This drill teaches the shuffle down the line of scrimmage, the sprint to the ball inside out, and the squaring up at the end to make the tackle.

We use a *downhill agility drill*, which teaches the rip and an angle tackle. We have a group of ballcarriers and linebackers in this drill. The coaches stand at the break dummy. The linebacker's dummies are aligned at an angle coming downhill to the ballcarrier. As the ballcarrier moves, the linebacker steps over the dummies. He is coming downhill to the break dummy where he buzzes his feet. The dummies he steps over are simulated blocks. We have blocker with arm shields to make the linebacker rip as he is coming downhill. We are ripping through those blocks. Once the linebacker gets to the break dummy, the back makes a cut off the dummy. The linebacker executes an angle tackle on the ballcarrier.

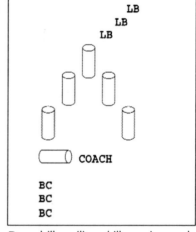

Downhill agility drill – rip angle tackle

The next drill is almost the same drill, but instead of the rip technique on the blocks we are playing a cut block. We don't do this drill every day except when we play teams like the Air Force Academy. When you play teams that are going to cut your linebacker, you better do these types of drills every day. That is the only way you can teach your players to stay on their feet. The object of a load-option football team is to knock everyone down. The drill is almost the same except for the dummy where the coach is positioned. That dummy makes the ballcarrier go one direction. At the end an angle tackle is executed.

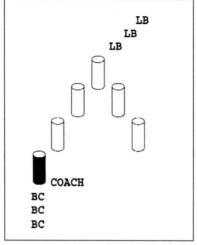

Downhill agility drill – cut angle tackle

When you teach *angle tackling*, everyone seems to have their own version of what and how they teach it. When I teach tackling I start backward. I start with a fit position of a perfect tackle. We get the hips sunk and the arms wrapped grabbing cloth. After we put them in the fit position, we back them off one step. We teach the lead step into the tackle. The lead step keeps the tackler from crossing his feet. We lead step right and lead step left and make a tackle going both ways. If the tackler gets into a crossover step, the ballcarrier has a distinct advantage. He can cut back on the tackler and run through him. If we are going to tackle with the right shoulder, the tackler takes a step with his right foot and leads with his left foot. On the left-shoulder tackle, he steps with his left foot and leads with his right foot. If the back cuts back, the tackler simply steps with his other leg and does not have to cross over. Great tacklers never have their feet together. You have to have them apart with a wide base.

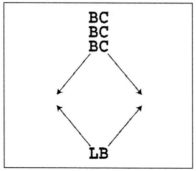

Angle tackle

The drill that teaches base is what we call the *hunter tackling drill*. Space five tube dummies three yards apart with a ballcarrier in each slot. In the first part of this drill, the linebacker shuffles down the line of dummies moving into each slot and making a form tackle on the ballcarrier. This allows him to make four form tackles. He shuffles into the first slot, makes the form tackle, recoils, and shuffles to the next slot and repeats the tackle. Each tackle is delivered with a shoulder tackle, wrap up, and extension lift. He repeats the drill four times.

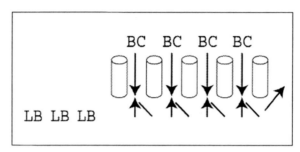

Hunter tackling drill – A

The second part of this drill is to align the ballcarriers in a line opposite the linebackers to the side of the dummies. On movement of the ballcarrier the linebacker begins to shuffle down the dummy. He keeps an inside-out angle on the ballcarrier. The ballcarrier can turn into any lane of dummies he chooses. The linebacker attacks the ballcarrier when he turns into a lane and makes a good angle tackle. This is a full-speed drill. If you want to add something to the drill, you can let the back one fake into the alleys. If he fakes into one alley he must run through the next one.

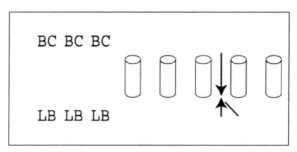

Hunter tackling drill – B

The first block protection drill we use is called the *cut drill* with an angle tackle. We line up four dummies with a line of linebackers. The blockers push the dummies at the feet of the linebacker as he shuffles down the line of dummies. The linebacker uses his hands to punch down on the dummies to keep them out of his feet. At the end of the dummy line he comes off and makes an angle tackle.

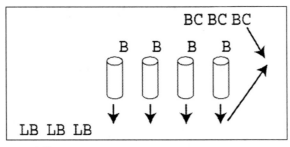

Cut drill

When we teach block protection, we teach what we refer to as hat and hands. This called the *rip drill*. We line up the offensive linemen in one line and the linebackers in the other line. We start out in a head-up position and work out to a shoulder position. The offensive lineman is using a scoop block. What we teach is *hat* in the V of the blocker's neck and *hand* underneath on the breastplate. We press off, lock out, and rip through with the inside arm. We use the rip to knock the offensive blocker's hands off the linebacker. He has to get off the block in a hurry and squeeze back into his gap responsibility. When we use this technique, I tell my linebacker to get off as quickly as he can, because that blocker is usually 320 pounds. Leverage is very important in this drill. We give the linebacker the option to come underneath the block if the lineman gives too much space upfield. However, that is a dangerous move if the lineman is quick.

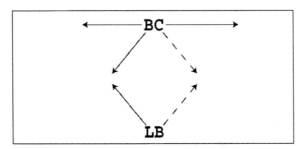

Rip drill

As the linebacker comes downhill on the scoop block, there is a point when he reaches the edge of the shoulder of the offensive guard, he has to rip through with his inside arm and not get pushed any wider. He has to squeeze back inside to keep the running lane at a minimum. Sometimes you have a linebacker who is a great athlete. We tell him to rip if he needs to, but if he doesn't, he goes to the ballcarrier. Coaching is great but you have to understand that sometimes ability takes over. Never take the athleticism away from the good athlete. If he can make the plays, let him make them. Of course, the opposite side of the coin is where his athleticism gets him in trouble. That is where the coach comes in and shows him how to play that area.

In the *down line shed drill*, the linebacker is playing off three blockers working downfield. We set up four dummies at an angle going downfield. We put three blockers and a ballcarrier in the slots of the dummies. He uses his shed techniques as he moves down the line and executes an angle tackle at the end.

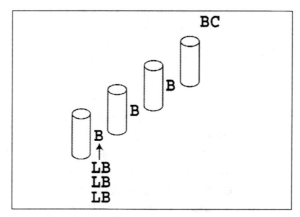

Down line shed drill

We use a *fit shed drill* to teach the proper fit on the offensive lineman. This is a simple drill. The linebacker fits into the block of the lineman, sheds him, and makes the tackle. We go right then left on this drill.

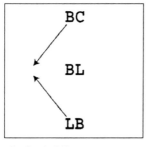

Fit shed drill

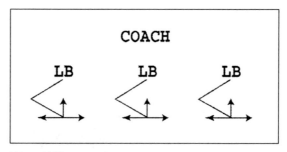

Wave drill at 45 degrees

I'm running out of time so I'll talk about these next two drills together. This is a pass-drop drill where we drop at 45-degree angles on the direction of the coach. The coach gives them two movements and makes the linebacker break up, left, or right.

In the second drill is called a *90-degree wave drill*. The linebacker tilts and runs straight back as if he is covering a tight end going vertical. At some point the coach levels the linebacker's retreat and makes him break left or right.

I'll briefly cover this next drill. I know you've seen it before so I won't talk too much about it. It is a simple drill that teaches linebackers their proper fit on flow. We line up

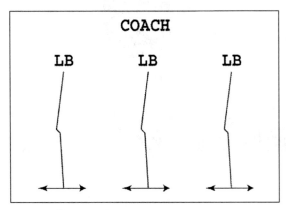

Wave drill at 90 degrees

an offensive line with one back five yards behind the center. All we do is give flow with the back; the linebackers react to the flow and make their fits to the line of scrimmage on the offensive blockers.

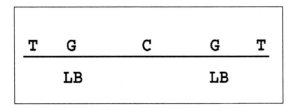

Read drill

Gentlemen, I appreciate you inviting me down here. I hope I gave you something you can use. If you get an opportunity to come to Notre Dame, make sure your drop in. I know I was going fast at the end, but if you want a copy of this tape I will make you a copy. Thank you very much.

15

Linebacker Techniques and Drills

Brock Spack
Purdue University
2001

I appreciate the Nike Coach of the Year Clinic inviting me to speak today. This is a great clinic. I spoke here nine or ten years ago. It is the best clinic I've ever been to. It is a privilege for me to be here. There are a lot of great coaches in the audience. I hope you learn something that can help you win a game or two.

I want to make sure we all understand what a positive influence a coach can have on a kid's life. All I ever wanted to be was a high school football coach because of my coach. But, I never became one. I played college and pro ball. When I got cut, I worked as a grad assistant in college and got into the rat race of Division I football.

My coach was real special in my life. I had good parents and grew up in a blue-collar industrial town in northern Illinois. Football was a big deal, and my parents wanted me to go to college. They wanted me to get an education. That kind of went in one ear and out the other. Fortunately, I had a guy who took me under his wing when I was 14. He showed me the way. He showed me I had to make my grades and be a student, as well as being a football player. He knew my goal was to some day play college football, and he was a huge influence on me.

When I signed my scholarship to go to Purdue, he pulled me aside, shook my hand, and made me promise to graduate in four years. I did that. He was a goal setter and a great motivator. The saddest day of my life was when he died. He was 37 years old and developed cancer. He died the year I was a senior in college. That was a tough year for me. Because of that guy, I got into coaching. He changed my whole life as to the way I looked at academics and football.

We are a 4-3 defense. Yours may not be a 4-3 type defense, but I'm going to talk about linebacker techniques in general. I'll give you some of the philosophy of why we do the things we do. Most of these ideas you can transfer over to any front or defense you play. I have a training tape to show you at the end.

The first point in our defensive philosophy is to be *aggressive*. We want our front to create a new line of scrimmage. We are an up-the-field team. We key the football and take as much of the line of scrimmage as we can with our down four guys.

The second thing is to *do what the players can do*. This year we were very young on defense. We started five freshmen in the Rose Bowl. We had nine freshmen on our two-deep depth chart. We didn't think we were going to win many games. We were hoping to get to six wins to qualify us for a bowl game. We were very fortunate to have some gifted players that came through for us. The freshman of the year in our conference was our free safety. But, we had to do what they could do. We have a lot of fancy zone pressure schemes we didn't use. We threw a lot of things at them in two-a-day practices to see what they could handle.

Physically, we could run. We were a fast team, and we set up the defense for speed. We are different than most of the teams in our league. We are fast and pretty undersized for the Big Ten. When you are thinking about schemes and techniques for your linebackers, make sure you do what they can do.

The third thing we want to do is to *be simple*. The more the offense does, the less we do. We play against one of the most complicated offenses in college football. We do it every day, in two-a-days, and in spring football. Our guys hate it, especially the linebackers, because they are playing out in space.

We live and die with *speed*. That is the fourth thing we talk about. That is critical for us, because we are playing with smaller players. We play with players who are fast or who play fast. Those things are different, but amount to the same thing. We tell our players, if they are not fast, they have to play fast. We made strides on defense this year because of that.

We want to *turn our players loose*. We don't try to bog them down with a lot of mental stuff. We keep it simple and turn them loose. We want our linebacker attacking the line of scrimmage and playing downhill. We want the ball to *go east and west*. We don't want the ball going north and south on us. We try to spill the ball to the outside and run it down with speed.

We try to promote an environment for success. We do it with five things. I have a coach assigned for every one of these points. I handle two of them. The first point is *pursuit*. We grade them on it and talk about it every day. We tell them what they did good and bad. It is the first thing we talk about on defense every day. The second point is *enthusiasm*. We coach it and grade them on it. We want to make sure our players are playing with a lot of emotion. The third thing is *turnovers*. This year was the best year we've had on defense statistically since we've been here at Purdue. Our total defense was up, but our turnovers were down. Our first three years, we either led the nation or were in the top 10 in forcing turnovers. This year we weren't as good. I can't explain that. We coach turnovers in practice and continually talk about it in practice. We work on tip drills, picking up fumbles, and all the drills relating to forcing turnovers.

The fourth thing in our philosophy is *tackling*. We tackle every day we are in full pads. That is critical. Our head coach is different than any head coach I've ever been around. During two-a-days practices, we have a live period every afternoon from 10 to 20 minutes. A lot of teams in college don't tackle live because they are worried about injuries. Our quarterback is live in some of our drills and that includes Drew Brees. Coach Joe Tiller lets us play football, because that is the way it will be played on Saturday. We scrimmage live situations every day we are in pads. Tackling is critical to a football team.

The fifth thing we talk about with our players is *soundness*. That, to us, is communication. It is alignment, assignment, and communication. That converts to the soundness of our defense. We go over these five things at the end of practice every day and give them a grade. We are a 4-3 defense because it allows our players to be aggressive in attacking the line of scrimmage. We play with smaller players.

Our system is easy to learn and play. That allows us to play these young kids. It lets them get on the field quicker. I don't think there has ever been a year quite like this one. I would have never believed we could win the Big Ten playing that many young players. We feel the 4-3 increases our sacks, because we are an up-the-field team and are very aggressive with our down four and our linebackers.

There are certain things we look for in our linebackers. First and foremost is *speed*. If he is not fast, he won't play fast. A lot of our linebackers are former safeties. We have two linebackers who were former receivers. Our starting Sam linebacker is a true freshman. He came in as a receiver. He came to Purdue thinking he was going to catch the ball. We moved him to linebacker after the first day. We play the fastest guys we can find at linebacker. I can only remember two guys in the last two years that played linebacker for us, who were linebackers in high school.

I want guys who have *quick feet*. When I evaluate a tape, I want to see a guy who has a great *motor*. When I talk about a motor, I'm talking about great effort. That is critical to any linebacker. I am looking for guys to play linebacker who have *explosive power*.

Linebackers must have *good football sense*. They have to be *tough*. They have to have a great *work ethic*. I feel linebackers work harder than anyone else. They must be *trustworthy*. I have to be able to trust them. They must have good *character*.

We have a philosophy for our linebackers. We want them to be aggressive and play downhill. We want them to make plays on the offensive side of the line of scrimmage. We express that to them in our meetings. We want them playing downhill on 45-degree angles. We want them to be big playmakers. It is critical for us to have our linebackers make big plays. We want them to play with great leverage and knee bend. A knee bender is a jaw breaker. We want our guys to bend their knees and strike on the rise. We want to keep it simple and create a language so we can communicate with them and make it easy for the players to understand.

What do we expect from our linebackers? We call it the "Three T's." The first *T* is *tempo*. We want them to play at a fast tempo. That is *how* we play. In individual periods, we hustle and play the game fast. The second *T* is *technique*. That is the *way* we play. We want to play with great technique. The third *T* is toughness. That is *what* we are. These are three things we emphasize in our individual periods with all our guys.

When you play with a 5.0 linebacker, he has to play fast. The first two years at Purdue, we had a couple of them. They played their butts off. They played fast and hustled all the time. We emphasize the tempo of our drills. I tell our coaches every day before we go out to practice: Do not forget what we are trying to get done. We have to develop and train our players to play fast. In every drill we do, I want those guys running fast. I want them to hustle and bust their butts.

When we teach our techniques, we break them down. We cover every small detail involved. We want them to understand the way we play. When we talk about toughness to our linebackers, we challenge them. This morning, for example, we ran 18, 180-yard conditioning intervals after we went through a 45-minute training circuit. We get our players up at 6:00 a.m. We put them through a good training period for an hour. It is tough. Today, we went more than an hour because they didn't finish on the sprint. Instead of running six 180's, we ran about 20. We want them perfect on sprinting.

We have a thought progression with our linebackers. If I put a new defense or stunt up on the board, I want them to go through this thought progression. The first thought should be "Where is my *stance* going to be?" If he is an inside linebacker, he is going to be in a two-point stance. If he's a linebacker outside the box, his stance changes. He has to know the stance he is playing and how he gets out of the stance. When we talk defense, we constantly talk about "pads out." We want the player's pads over his toes. That is where we want them in a hitting position.

The second thing is *alignment*. We have a very easy alignment system. We number our front alignments 0 to 7. If the alignment is off the line of scrimmage, we add a zero in front of the alignment. A linebacker aligned on the outside shoulder of the offensive guard would be in a "03" alignment.

The third thing is *footwork*. That is getting out of our stance. I'll show you some tape in a minute that will demonstrate this. We have a thing we do, especially with young players. It is called popping our feet. This helps us eliminate false steps.

The fourth thing is *technique*. We label all our techniques, especially for our linebackers. If our Will linebacker is playing in the B gap, we call that a *B-window technique*. The Mike linebacker who has the A gap, we call that a *stack technique*. The Sam linebacker playing in the C gap, we call a *C-window technique*.

The fifth thing is *responsibility*. Within every technique, there are responsibilities. On every play, there are three things the linebacker has to know: run to, run away, or pass. He has to know what he is going to do on each of those situations. It is pretty simple and easy. Obviously, it gets more complicated than that when we break it down. If I am a B-window player, our primary keys are the backs, and the secondary keys are the linemen. If I am a linebacker out of the box, my primary key becomes the uncovered lineman. That tells us if it is run or pass faster than a back would.

We have five things that are important in our individual drills. They are movement, defeating blocks, tackling, play recognition, and pass drops. In our movement drills, we use bags and cones. We always incorporate some kind of football skill with those movement drills. We tackle coming off a bag drill. We defeat a cut blocker coming off a bag. We dip and rip with our outside arm coming off a bag. We plant the hands coming off the bag. We want to do some kind of football skill coming off a bag, dummy, or cone.

We take on blockers different ways. On direct blocks, we dip and rip, taking them on with our forearms. On indirect blocks, we play with our hands. We tackle every day, and I'll show you some of these tackling drills later.

We use key drills for play recognition and pass drops. I break this down by technique. We are a pattern read defense as far as zone goes. We run pattern read drills every day in our individual drills.

The big question I get in most clinics is how we read and key. We have a simple system. I don't want a linebacker to be a robot. We have become multiple over the years. We can't just line up in a 4-3 and survive. We have to change up our fronts. Because of that, I went to this system. I stole this from the Jacksonville Jaguars. When you watch the tape, this will make sense to you.

We label points on the defense as to where the linebacker should fit on flow. It relates to the angle of flow the linebacker reads. The point over the ball is the *inside point*. The point between the guard and tackle is the *base point*. The point in the C gap is *outside point*. The C-window technique has an outside fill or outside scrap. The reason we do this is to keep the linebacker from being a robot. I don't want the linebacker running to the B gap just because the ball is run at him. If the ball is not in the B gap, I don't want him in there. Understanding our key drill is critical to understanding these points on the defense.

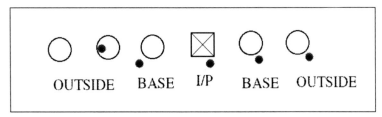

Points on defense

There are four angles of flow by the offensive backs that our linebackers must recognize. The first flow is a tight dive off the hip of the center. If the Will linebacker is getting a tight dive away, he is a B-window player. His angle of flow on tight dive away is inside point, which is over the center. He is not flowing into the B gap. The Mike linebacker is mirroring the angle of the back. On the tight dive off the hip of the center, the Mike linebacker hits the A gap like he is going to blitz. If he hits the A gap, and the window closes, he scrapes over the top of his 3 technique.

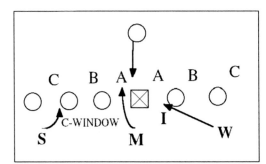

Tight dive angle

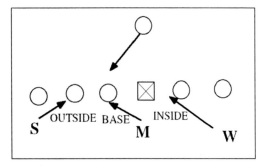

Dive angle

The next back flow is the dive angle. If the Mike linebacker reads the angle of the back toward the dive, his angle is a 45-degree angle to clear the 3 technique. The Will linebacker on dive angle away still has inside point. The Sam linebacker reads dive angle toward him. He is the C-window player. He has to read the window and see whether it is opened or closed. If it is closed, he has the outside point scrape. If it is open, he attacks the back.

The next angle is the power angle flow. The Will linebacker has power angle away. He works for the inside point all the way to the opposite base point. His footwork will change somewhat. He stays flatter so he can clear the guard-center area. That is the area we call the *hump*. He checks the hump, then works downhill to the base point.

The Sam linebacker is keying the C window. If the window opens, he fills right now on an outside fill point. If the window is closed, he outside scrapes off the butt of the defensive end. The Mike linebacker mirrors the angle of the back. He is generally attacking at a 45-degree angle. He attacks the base point to the outside fill point.

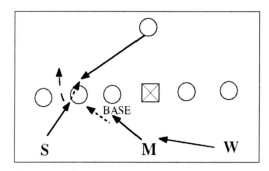

Power angle

The next flow is sweep angle, or what many people call *fast flow*. The Will linebacker on sweep angle away takes a flatter step and runs the hump. That means he is going to give a little ground. He works over the top of the inside point to the guard-tackle box. When he reaches that point, he gets downhill. The Mike linebacker clears the tackle and box, and gets downhill. The Sam linebacker plays off the offensive end. He is reading the flow of the tackle. If the tackle is fighting to reach, the Sam fills inside.

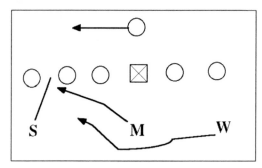

Sweep angle

We create a language by using those points. This language makes it real easy for our linebackers to understand what you want them to do. This has been really good for us. When we played true freshmen who had never played the position, this made it easy for them.

Let's get into the tape now. We are a 4-3 alignment and our linebackers are quite deep. We play them with their heels at five yards from the line of scrimmage. The reason we play them so deep is to get them downhill with force.

There are things we look for in our stance. We want the pads out, which I talked about before. We want the chin up with a nice flat back. He has his toes slightly in and his heels slightly out. He has a slight bend in his knees with a good power angle in his knees and ankles. His feet should be flat on the ground, but we want the weight on the inside. His elbows are tight inside. We put our hands on the thigh pads, but never on the knees. The reason we want the elbows inside is to create power. If you put your elbows outside, you can't push. That lets us dip and rip, because the elbows are tight to the body.

This is a little drill we call "popping our feet." I got this from a high school coach in Texas. This keeps us from taking a false step. We play so fast downhill we want our linebackers to give a slight pop of the feet. Instead of wasting motion by jumping forward or backward, we pick the foot up and almost put it down in the same position. We can do this drill mirroring a back or lineman. In the dive angle, the linebacker pops his feet and then gets into his 45-degree angle run.

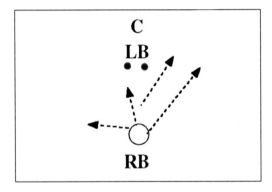

Foot pop

We want the shoulders down. We don't want to travel with our shoulders out of our stance. The critical part of a linebacker is getting out of his stance. I don't want him to raise or lower his shoulders as he moves. We always want his pads over his toes. We drill our angles without linemen to start with. They simply mirror the angle of the backs they are keying. They know their points by the angle of the backs.

When we teach our linebackers, they have to know whether we are playing an eight- or seven-man structure defense. If it is seven-man structure defense, the backside linebacker is shuffling. If it is an eight-man structure, he is running.

The Mike linebacker has inside point on the tight dive. He has the base point on a dive angle. He has outside point on the power angle. We don't use the term *wrong-arm*. We call it *win inside*. We want the defender to take on the block with his outside arm and kick the blocker's butt. On the dive angle, if the Sam linebacker reads the C window open, he attacks the back in the hole. The Mike linebacker reads the base point and plays over the top of the Sam linebacker, who has closed the window.

On the next drill, we put linemen into the key drill. That gives the linebacker a cluttered picture. We are doing the same drill as we did without the line, but now they are seeing blocks. In every drill we do, we emphasize eyes up.

We do all kinds of ladder drills for footwork. We use form-tackling drills with a three-step movement. The approach is the first phase. The fit-up is the second phase. It is important in the fit-up position to squeeze your elbows together. He has to snap and roll his hips in the third phase of the drill. We approach the tackle under control, fit into a good position, and explode and lift to finish the tackle.

We use a drill that we call the *door drill*. We put a cone in the middle and align a back and linebacker on either side five yards from the cone. The manager is the door. He stands over the cone in the middle. A lot of linebackers are not tall guys, and it is hard for them to see. The back takes two steps toward the door and breaks to one side or the other of the door. The linebacker takes two steps and reacts to the direction of the back, looking for the opposite-colored jersey. Once he sees it, he lowers his pads, makes the hit, and drives him backwards.

A drill we like to run is our drop-and-tackle drill. We have the linebacker spot drop to an area on the field. He takes a good 45-degree drop to a cone, which is about eight yards deep. We have a back standing next to the quarterback. Once the linebacker reaches the cone, the back can break into a flare pattern. The quarterback throws the ball and the linebacker reacts up to make the tackle. The linebacker works on driving on the ball and attacking from the inside out.

We use sleds and bags to work on playing off blocks. When you play off blocks, we want everything going forward. I don't want to see any body parts going out. We hit everything on a rise. We step with the inside arm and leg. If you are watching a boxing match, you never see a fighter throw a jab with his left hand without stepping with his left foot. We want to step and keep our leverage. We want our pad level under the level of the blocker. On contact, we want to roll the wrist out and swing the off hand through. I tell them it is like looking at your watch. At impact, we want the feet on the ground. We dip and rip and get underneath the blocker. We can do all these drills on a sled, as well as with bags.

When we play with our hands, we want to play with our hands above our eyes. We strike and hit on a rise. When the backside linebacker is playing the inside point, he is playing with his hands. We want good fast hands with the elbows always inside. If he rolls his hips too much while he is playing with his hands, he has a tendency to get locked into the block. We want the hips to stay behind during this drill. We want their palms together with their thumbs up. Once we get on a block, we work on turning the blocker's shoulders. We want to push with one hand and pull with the other.

Gentlemen, I appreciate your time. Thank you.

16

Linebacker Fundamentals

Lou Tepper
University of Illinois
1996

It is a three-and-a-half hour drive from Champaign to Louisville. It just took me five-and-a-half hours to fly here. It was a tough flight, but I am glad to be with you today. I would say that in my 29 years of coaching, there is not another topic that I would prefer to speak on than linebackers. I have been blessed in my career to have some great linebackers. I am going to give you some of the things I've learned along the way. I think these things are very fundamental.

Regardless of scheme, there are four things a linebacker has to do. It doesn't matter whether you are running a 4-3 or a multiple-reduction front like we play. We have been in that front for 19 years. If your linebackers can do these four things, they can play in any scheme. A linebacker has to hit and shed, pursue, tackle, and have coverage skills. In our scheme, he has to have 90 percent zone skills and 10 percent man skills. If he can do those four things, he can play anywhere and in any scheme. If you agree with that, then *movement* becomes essential.

Movement is the key to playing linebackers, not size. Of the 16 first-round picks I've had, eight of them were under 210 pounds when they left me. When I began coaching in a Division II school in 1968, we had 210-pound linemen and 210-pound linebackers. The big change in the last 30 years is that we face linemen in the 280-pound range. We recruited a guy this year who is 6'8" and 370 pounds, who is an offensive lineman. Linebackers haven't changed in what is required of them and movement is still the skill that is required of them. If you put a 300-pound guard over a 250-pound linebacker, the guard will not sweat. But if you put that guard over a 210-pound linebacker, the guard will sweat bullets. These four things don't have anything to do with size. The hit-and-shed is the only one that puts the linebacker at any disadvantage at all. But it is not as much as you might think. Those are the basics by which we go. Therefore, our linebackers are down-sized as linebackers go in our league.

To identify linebackers, we use four tests. None of these tests have anything to do with height or weight. The first test is the 40-yard dash. I'm not here to tell you the 40 is the right test for a linebacker's speed, but I know the difference in speeds. I know the difference between a 4.88 and a 4.8. The second test is what we call the *jingle-jangle* or *shuttle run*. It is a 20-yard run. We put the linebacker straddling a line. He moves five yards to his left, touches a line, sprints 10 yards the other way, touches the line, and finishes across the line where he started. We compare his shuttle-run time to his 40-yard time. If the shuttle time is 0.4 to 0.5 under the 40 time, he probably has the change of direction to play linebacker.

There have been some great examples of that. I was at Virginia Tech under Bill Dooley. We had a guy by the name of Mike Johnson. He is finishing his tenth year of playing linebacker in the NFL. He came to us as a middle guard. His change of direction was so good, we moved him to linebacker. He started as a true freshman. When I went to Colorado, we tested everyone. We had a walk-on from another division who transferred and walked on. He was 5'10" and weighed 280 pounds. He was playing offensive guard. We tested him in the shuttle. He ran the fastest time of all the linemen in our program. We told him if he would lose weight, he had a chance to play defense. He had never played defense before. We got him down to 240 pounds, and the next year he was an All-Big Eight noseguard. This is a great test. The NFL uses it now.

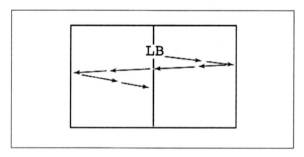

The third test is the *power* or *hang clean*. When you deal with linebackers who are that much smaller than the guys they are lining up across from, this becomes extremely important. The first four linebackers I had play in the NFL, the only test that they ranked first on was the clean.

The fourth thing we test is body fat. We test them about three times a year for body fat. Brownlow was with us in 1986. He called himself 6'0", but he was about 5'9". He weighed 248 pounds and thought he was the meanest man around. He could play hard for about 20 plays. But he couldn't play 70 plays and another 20 plays on special teams. The next year, as a sophomore, I got him down to 224 pounds, and he was All-Big Ten. His body fat went from 28 percent down to 14 percent. What we look for are guys in the 12- to 15-percent range. If you have a linebacker whose body fat is in the high teens, he cannot play linebacker. He cannot play hard for the entire game. If you are counting on him to be a great pursuit guy, he cannot do it. If you have one who is 20 percent body fat, forget it. He will let you down when you need him.

I look at the 40 for speed, the change of direction for pursuit and tackling, the clean for his ability to shed, and the body fat to see how long he can last. One of the best linebackers I ever had played for me at Colorado. He ran the 40 in 5.18. That was last of all the 60 linebackers who tried out for the NFL. But he was third in the shuttle run with a 4.33. The difference between his 40 time and shuttle was 0.8, which was why he was a great linebacker.

When I started coaching, I thought stance was a big deal. I made every guy have the same stance with his hands in the same place. I don't anymore. What we stress now is the *base*. Most linebackers want to get a wide base and get real low. The first thing those linebackers have to do to move is narrow their base. We play our linebackers at a four-yard depth. I want his feet under his armpits. We watch our linebackers on tape. If they step under themselves to move, we narrow their base. I want his hands lightly on his thighs and looking right through his keys. I used to have the linebackers hang their hands between their legs, and some still do that. The only thing I tell them now is not to get too much pressure on their hands. The height of the stance depends on the depth of the linebacker. The closer to the line of scrimmage the linebacker plays, the lower his stance has to be.

With the *pre-snap keys*, the linebacker can find out a lot. One thing the linebacker coach should do is study splits between the linemen. I think they are very telling in three of our 11 games every year. We find teams that spread us out to run inside plays and tighten down to run outside. With those keys, you see our linebacker depths vary. We start at four yards. If the line splits are tight, we back up to five. If the line splits are big, we move up to three yards and tighten. You can take advantage of that if you and your players watch line splits.

On the college level, I think one of the worst things being taught is offensive line stances. We are doing so much on offense that some of us have backed away from fundamentals. If three teams tell us something from their splits, there are at least eight of the 11 teams that tell us a great deal from their stances. The running game today has become simplistic and is not as difficult to defend as it once was. We used to get a lot of scheme blocking. We got G-pulls, powers, and two or three different trap blocks. Today, we are facing so many teams in the one-back set who are running nothing but the zone play and a simple trap. There is not much in their offense except four or five base runs. By watching the stance of linemen, we know the running play before it is run. We have a coded word for the stances we see. If both guards are in a run stance, we know we are facing an inside zone play. We communicate that up and down the line. If we have one guard in a run stance and one in a pull stance, we know the play is a counter and we know the direction it is going. When both guards are in a soft or pull stance, it is usually draw or pass.

We teach our linebackers *down-and-distance*. One of the things that make me fume in practice is a kid who doesn't know the down-and-distance. We constantly drill that. We have one linebacker who is trained in down-and-distance. While the other linebacker is getting the signal for the defense, he is calling the down-and-distance. He will call, "Second-and-two, waste down." He is trained so that every down-and-distance, he has a tendency to tell the defense at that point.

The linebacker who calls the signals stands on the edge of the huddle. The down-and-distance linebacker is in front of the huddle. How many times in college or pro games have you seen the guy calling the defense getting ticked off because the signal has not come in from the bench when he is ready? He gets anxious, curses, pulls on his headgear, and is really ticked. I don't want that in front of our defensive huddle. If he is going to get anxious, I want him on the edge of the huddle. With the offensive personnel changes that offenses go through, I hold my call until I know what offense is in the game. Once I give the call, the signal linebacker steps to the front of the huddle and gives the call with confidence. I want that signal caller enthusiastic. If we give a bad call and the linebacker is jacked up and enthusiastic, there is a good chance something good will happen. If he is not, then everyone in that huddle sees the call in the linebacker's eyes. If he is positive, then everyone sees that too.

This next part of the lecture is the single most important thing I'm going to tell you tonight. I think fundamentals are the most poorly coached thing today, dealing with linebackers. The first fundamental is called *hit-and-shed*. That is taking on a blocker. When you take on a blocker, the number one issue is the base. That is true of almost every position that is played. There are three different bases to take on the blocker. The first way is with the opposite foot and body position. When we coach this part, we hardly talk about the upper body. We talk about the feet. It doesn't matter whether you are a flipper, hands, or shoulder player. If your feet are wrong, you lose. If the linebacker takes on a blocker with his right shoulder with his left foot forward, he gets turned. Not once in a while, but every time. I did this in my linebacker drills at Virginia Tech and Colorado, when my son was young. I had my linebackers stand with their left foot in advance of the right foot. I brought my 10-year-old son into the drill and had him push on their right shoulders. Every one of them turned.

The second way and correct way to take on a blocker is with the same contact area and foot forward. If a linebacker is taking the blocker on with his right shoulder, his right foot should be forward. That is the strongest position he can get into. That is the most dramatic thing you have to present to your linebackers. It is the same thing for your defensive linemen. A lot of the 300-pounders in our league are soft. If that 210-pound linebacker will stick his foot in the ground, get his pad under the pad of the lineman, he will win that battle time after time.

The third way to take on the block is a guy who is trying to do what you tell him. He moves forward with the correct foot forward, but just before contact he has it off the ground. When that happens, he gets pancaked. When I find a guy who does that, I pick him up, pat him on the back, and tell him he is only a short distance from being successful. All he has to do is get his foot down, planted, with the weight over the front foot, and he will win. I would much rather see this happening than opposite foot and shoulder. Opposite foot and shoulder will never win.

If you talk to a lot of linebacker coaches, they tell you the same thing. But they don't demand it from their players. We do this every day of every practice with the exception of Monday and Friday during the season. We spent time every day of every practice on hit-and-shed. We have about 50 drills where we take on a blocker. I'll tell you about a couple of them. One, I told you about with my son. Another is done on air. We put them in a stance and simply say "Hit." They take their short step with the proper foot and roll the hips. If the step is too long, they can't roll the hips. They take a short step, get the foot planted, and explode the hips. You have to settle the weight over the front foot. We can't run through a blocker. If you play your linebackers on only the left or right, you could work on just one side. We flip our linebackers, so we work on both sides.

In our scheme, we play with the linebacker's inside foot on the outside foot of the guard, four yards deep. When the guard comes out, we don't try to run through him. If we do, we lose. I don't tell them they have to move two yards or any distance. The thing I want to coach is that just before contact, the linebacker has to have his foot planted so he can explode like a missile off the base with my pad under his pad. That is easy now. The offensive linemen are so tall we have no trouble getting pad under pad. We practice this on a sled. We get one step from contact, step, and explode into the sled. We do it over and over until it becomes second nature. We use an old statement: "If you throw a cat up in the air, he lands on his feet. If you throw a linebacker up in the air, he lands with his hit foot forward." Hip roll can be developed in the weight room, and it is a key issue. The base must be short so the hips can come through clean. He has to have strong hips. If he will do that, the small linebacker can take on blockers.

The second fundamental is *pursuit*. Pursuit really ties in with taking on blockers. There are three types of pursuit that we stress. The first one is *shuffle*. This is a universal term for linebackers. I don't know if all of you understand why we use this term. The shuffle is when the ball is moving from tackle to tackle. That is the only time I want them to shuffle. The shuffle keeps the linebacker behind the ball while it is moving slow. The most important thing is the shuffle always keeps the linebacker only one step away from a perfect base. If the linebacker turns his feet and crosses over and has to take on a blocker, he has no chance. That is why we shuffle. We never cross our feet from tackle to tackle, unless the ball has been tossed. This also lets the linebacker change direction and still be only one step away from a perfect base.

The second type of pursuit is called *alley*. We use this pursuit when the ball is moving with speed from the tight end to the sideline. He shuffles first. But when he knows the ball is a perimeter play, he turns his hips and runs. He runs as fast as he can, but works his arms to try and keep his shoulders as parallel to the line of scrimmage as he can. When the linebacker is shuffling, he wants to stay on the backside hip of the ball and say, "Please cut back." On the alley, he is still behind the ball, but because it is moving so much faster, he stays three yards behind the ball. If I am on the hip and the ballcarrier turns up, the linebacker will never make the play. From the three yards behind, he can turn, square his hips, and make the tackle. We have a statement that I make our kids complete. I start out by saying, "The longest runs in football _____," and they have to complete the sentence. They should answer "break behind the backside linebacker." I challenge you to take all the runs of 20 yards or more and put them on one reel of film. I would bet the vast majority of them are right behind the backside linebacker. If you want to cut down on big runs, discipline the backside linebacker to stay behind the ball.

The third pursuit is probably the most important. That is what we term *press*. This is how we define it. When the linebacker is shuffling or playing the alley, and he sees an opening to the ball, he goes after the ball. Press upfield hard. I used to think when I first started coaching that it was natural. Guys either had it or they didn't. Now I believe you can train guys to press the ball. In all the drills that we do for the linebacker, it is not complete until the linebacker presses. If he is shuffling, he has to press the first open seam. We condition our linebacker to press. Sometimes you will see our linebacker press on a sweep away from him. He shouldn't, because the ball is too far away from him. I don't even get on them about it. You never want to take the stinger away from a linebacker for pressing the ball. We are an ultimate read defense. We finished third in the nation on defense in 1989 and blitzed only 11 times the entire season. We had more minus plays by linebackers in the Big Ten. The reason for that is our kids are taught to shuffle and press.

Pursuit is 93 percent. We grade every play on defense for pursuit. From the time the ball is snapped until it is over, our defense has to be in pursuit. We grade our linebackers on the frontside and the backside with two separate grades for both run and pass. The pursuit grade is shared with everyone. We tell them if they are below 93 percent, they are on probation. If it happens two weeks in a row, they are on the bench. You have to have guts to do that to your best players. The purpose is to convince them to go hard all the time. If they do that in a 70-play game, they have a chance to make a big play one time. One big play is no big deal. But 11 big plays is a big deal. We grade pursuit in everything we film. Defensive backs should be held to a higher account. They should have 97 percent. The defensive line should be a little lower. They should score about 90 percent. When the team score is 93 percent, we don't lose many games. Their names go on the chart for all to see. If two guys did not give the effort, everyone can see it. If it happens the next week, they don't start.

I don't believe our tackling is much different from anybody else. I won't spend a lot of time on it. I can tell you the important thing in tackling is *vision*. You have to have your eyes on the breastplate of the ballcarrier. The *hat placement* is on the ball. We try to put our forehead on the ball and punch it out with the immediate tackle. Anyone who comes after that tries to strip the ball. *Forward lean* is important, particularly in our league. We have a lot of big backs in the Big Ten. We have to *wrap up* with both arms.

The last thing you have to have is a *wide base*. That is particularly important in short-yardage plays. We do short-yardage drills because almost everyone in our league has spin backs. Those are backs who make contact at the line of scrimmage, then spin. The down-and-distance linebacker in short yardage keeps a wide base. When the linebacker fronts up the back, if his base is too narrow, he will turn.

I am a defensive head coach. Whenever we go together in a 7-on-7, 9-on-7, or team drill, the defense always fronts up. The hair on the back of my neck stands up when we let somebody run through our defense. If we have a 7-on-7 drill and the wide receiver catches a curl, and he is going down to score, the defensive backs go with him. We front up the receiver. It is not a live tackle. The first guy there fronts up the ballcarrier, and everyone else tries to strip the ball. The offensive man gets to make them miss and they have to protect the ball. So it works well for both sides. We never come low on defense, but we want all the defense coming.

We try to keep *zone coverages* simple. When we recognize pass from the guards, the linebackers yell it out. The danger is the play-action pass. We retreat at a 45-degree angle. A lot of people teach their linebackers to backpedal. The advantage of a linebacker who backpedals is the ability to make a three-way break on the ball. He can break left, right, and forward. When we open up at the 45-degree angle, we can only break the way we are opened up. We do that because that is the fastest way to gain depth. When the quarterback pulls up, the linebacker pulls up. We try to eliminate drift by the linebacker.

Drift, to us, is the movement the linebacker makes after the quarterback pulls up. If the linebacker continues to move after the quarterback has pulled up, he is cheating. The only way he can intercept the ball is toward the direction he is moving. He can't break on the throw underneath or inside. There are some exceptions to this rule. One of those exceptions is third and 15 to go. If we give that up, we are dummies. What we do is open at the 45-degree angle, square up, and drift backward to the area we are going to give the offense. Then we work back up to stop the first down. We want to get deep, force the offense to throw underneath, and come up to make the tackle. What kills me is the linebacker who jumps the drag route on a third-and-20 and lets the offense throw the square in behind him for the first down. Every drag pattern is generally accompanied by a high-low pattern off the linebacker. We teach the linebacker to open at the 45-degree angle. If he reads the drag, he lets it go and begins to drift. To him, drag means drift. We want him drifting under the pattern forming behind him. In the two-minute drill, we also allow them to drift.

The last thing in zone coverage is 93 percent pursuit. When the ball is thrown to the post, we don't expect our player to look at the ball. We expect him to turn and sprint to the ball. If you force the linebacker to run after the deep pass, something good will come from it. It is an attitude. When the defense makes big plays from doing what you ask them to do, you have got to promote that. Put it in a "Big Hit" film and things like that.

Man-to-man coverage is hard. I will not spend a lot of time on this because I am not an expert on this subject. We use the man a few times a game. If we play 70 plays and are in man coverage five times, that is a lot for us. Usually when we show a blitz, the quarterback is smiling because he knows it is a bluff. There are three things we teach: First, we *deny all inside breaks*. We take our nearside foot and hand in this technique. We put our foot down the middle of the receiver and our hand right on the sternum. Second, if the receiver goes vertical, the linebacker turns and *chews ear*. That means he turns and runs, looking through the inside ear hole of the headgear. We never allow the inside break.

Third, on the flat route, we play *underneath the receiver*. We don't play over the top. We want our hat between the quarterback and the receiver. We accelerate to the flat route and get under it. We feel the hardest throw in a blitz situation is the flat throw. The linebacker doesn't look back at the quarterback. He gets his hat on the downfield hip of the flat receiver and runs. The quarterback sees the hat of the linebacker and knows if he underthrows the ball, he has a chance of giving up six points. The quarterback doesn't know we are not going to look back. Most of the throws are overthrows.

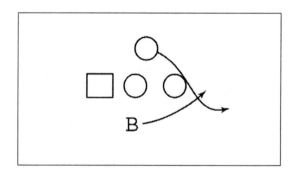

Our *pre-practice work* with our linebackers is extremely important. We meet for 30 minutes to an hour, depending upon the day. We have a tip sheet prepared for every Tuesday, Wednesday, Thursday, and Friday practice. That is a must for all coaches. They put the meeting plans and diagrams on the blackboard. I don't want to walk into one of my coach's meetings and find nothing there. The ideal coach has a tip sheet for the players when they walk in. He has highlighted it so they can make notes on their sheets. He has his stuff on the board so they are ready to go. And he's got his tape on the machine, ready to go. I hate to walk into a coach's meeting and he is fumbling around trying to find something. You don't have a 20-hour week like we do. If we have 30 minutes to meet, I want 30 minutes of meeting. I don't want 25 minutes of meeting and five minutes of putting things up on the board or finding tape. The coach has to be a teacher. That's what coaching is all about. You have to tell them. Read with them. Show them on tape. Make them verbalize the material. Have your players use all their senses.

I believe that great teachers *eliminate gray areas*. If we can eliminate the gray areas, players will perform extremely well. You will not believe this, but our inside linebacker has played 800 snaps and played one technique. Our eagle linebacker will play two techniques, and one of them is a long-yardage technique where he doesn't have to be great against the run. He has a key that tells him what to do. There are only five things that he has to do. For 20 minutes each day, he does those things for five years. The inside linebacker has eight things to do, depending on what his guard tells him. Some of those things are gray. That is where you have to be a great teacher. As an example, the guard block down means a lot of things. It could be isolation, veer option, or maybe a scoop. The coach that can make those blocks understandable to his linebacker can be a great linebacker coach.

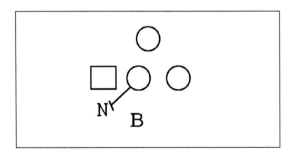

Your kids want to be good. *Be demanding* and make them do it exactly right. In 29 years, I've never cursed one of my players on the field. I've never grabbed them by the face mask. I have never called them a jerk. It's just not my style. I think linebackers are the toughest guys in the world. But we are positive when we work with them. I played for a guy named Dewey King. He is in his eighties, and we still talk with great regularity. Dewey said if you call a kid a dog long enough, he'll be one. I've watched practices in the NFL and other colleges. I can tell you there are some tough S.O.B.

coaches out there. They are not all bad, but some of them have made dogs out of players because they don't believe in their players. I'll tell you what Dewey did for me. When I left college, I felt I was the best college corner that had ever played the game. I wasn't even close to being that, but I believed it.

The way we do it now is like Dewey did it. If a kid does something right, we pat him on the back and say "nice job." If he does it aggressively, you get them and say "great job." When they do something wrong, this is what we do. We tell them, "Great job, but if you do this one thing differently, you have got it. Don't get tired of me making you do it over and over again until you get it exactly right. Doing it almost right isn't good enough. You have to do it exactly right."

Let me show you what we do in Tuesday and Wednesday practice during the season. We work on our special teams first. The punt is the most important play in football, and we spend 10 minutes each day on that. We have two other kicking areas we work on for a total of 25 minutes for our special. We have a tempo period at least once and usually twice during the week. We work three minutes on agilities. That is some form of pursuit. Then we have four minutes of team pursuit. The offense does their agilities and team takeoffs during these periods. Then we come together at the 50-yard line. We divide up into four groups: running backs, tight ends, and receivers against defensive backs, and other defensive personnel. In the groups, we tackle. It is the longest two minutes of their life. We simply have two lines facing each other. The runner can go five yards either way, down the line. The linebacker is going to shuffle and press. We want the back to protect the ball and get into the linebacker hard like a short-yardage run. We don't take anyone down to the ground. They are high-collision runs. The linebackers are trying to flatten out the ballcarrier, and the ballcarrier tries to move forward. In those four groups and two minutes, there are 200-plus tackles. That is our best tackling work during the week.

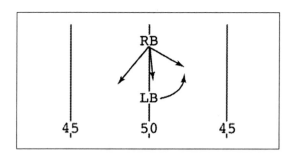

From there, we go to ABCs for 10 to 15 minutes after tempo. During this time, we emphasize taking on the blocker. That is the fundamental period of hit-and-shed. After that, we go to a technique period for 20 minutes per day. We demand they do it right. During the 20 minutes, we limit the drill to one technique. We go over and over and watch their confidence soar.

We go to the group period next. We spend 10 minutes in what we call *key and perimeter*. We run perimeter runs against the strong safeties and outside linebackers. Sometimes we stick the 5-technique tackle in there. From there, we go to a 9-on-7 middle drill where we run nothing but inside plays. It is the most important 20 minutes for us during the day. For us, it is the only live period we have all day. Normally, we do 10 minutes against our offense and 10 minutes against a scout offense. It is high intensity. In a 10-minute period, we get about 14 plays.

After that, we go to a 7-on-7 for 20 minutes. This is a grade pursuit period. Every guy has to fly to the ball. We do four plays in a row. When we get guys going full-tilt for four plays, we increase to five plays. It is rare for us to get over eight in a row at that intensity.

When we go to the team period, here are the things we work on. We seldom run an inside play. The exception might be the draw. The reason for that is the draw is not a good play to run in the 9-on-7 period. We run play-action pass and perimeter runs in team drill. Any adjustments we have, we run during the team period.

Thanks for being here. I enjoyed talking to you.

17

Linebacker Drills and Techniques

Gregg Williams
Houston Oilers
1997

I appreciate the opportunity to visit with you. I want to make this as informative as I can. I want to make this as fun as I can. I understand that it is a poor meeting when I'm doing all the talking. I feel that same way when I am involved with the players. A meeting has to be an extension of the field. I don't play anymore. They do. They play the games on Sunday, Saturday afternoons, and Friday nights. They have to know as much about what you do so that they are better able to play the game.

One of the most complimentary things that can be said about me is, "You still think like a high school coach." That is still said about me when I get into the personnel meetings on whether a guy can play or not. Right now, we are going through all that with the college draft. If the kid makes plays at the high school level, he'll make plays at the college level, if given a chance to play. If the guy is a playmaker at the college level, he will make plays at our level, too. It will happen that way because playmakers are playmakers. Some of the best football coaches I have ever coached with to this day were the high school coaches that I played for, the high school coaches on my staff, and the coaches that are still there in Kansas City.

It was easier for me to get on with the Houston Oilers than it was for me to become a head football coach in the state of Texas. I do think that there are some great high school football coaches in Texas. Some of the worst coaches I've been associated with are at the pro level. There are some weak coaches in pro ball. There are some baby-sitters here. They think the guys can go ahead, line up, and play. All they have to do is keep them out of trouble and make sure his car gets washed. It doesn't happen that way. These guys still have to be coached. They crave to be coached. We are going to coach them from when they get out of the Lexus until they get back into it at the end of the day. That is the kind of staff Jeff Fisher has put together.

Before I get long and drawn out with a lot of things dealing with linebacker play, I'm going to hit this really quick. I'm going to talk about philosophy. I would much rather be sitting where you are than doing this. That is what I have missed for the last 10 years since I've been at this level. I miss the clinics, fellowship, and the interchange of ideas. Understand, at the pro level, we don't tell anybody crap. We don't tell each other anything, because that is taking food out of my kid's mouth. The guys that will get me fired are the guys at the Chargers, Lions, and Cowboys. We are not telling anybody anything. When I sat out there, I used to hate all that philosophical bullcrap. I will be brief with this.

I do believe this. If you are a young football coach, the most important thing in coaching is your philosophy, not your scheme. It is more about changing the behavior of that young man than it is about that scheme. I do believe it is important. That is why I'm going to talk a little about this to start with. After that, I'll get into some drills. I've got a film at the end that I'll show. After you watch that film, you're going to say, "He ain't any better than me." I am you. I have coached junior high, high school, college, and pro football. The reason I'm still at this level is because I'm going to coach the players every single day as hard as I can coach them.

I had a guy say to me, "You need to understand: I'm an individual. You need to treat me as an individual." He needed to understand to do it our way. We had to give him more than one way to be successful. But if he thought about being an individual, he needed to go to an individual sport. This is a team sport.

Let's talk really quickly about linebackers. I've done this at every level I've been at. As soon as the game is over, I come in and turn the film on. I ask myself two questions. The first question is, "Am I coaching that specific technique?" I ask that question especially if there was a bad play or something negative that happened. I'm going to study that play and find out how and why it broke down. If I'm the problem, I have to change it. I have to go back and find a better technique to allow that kid to be successful. If the answer to question number one is no, then I ask question number two. If I'm not coaching that technique, I must be allowing it to happen over and over again because I'm seeing that same stuff week after week. That's it. If you will live by that creed, you will start to see a change in your players.

I talk in clinics across the country. I talk to corporations, businessmen, salesmen, coaches, and players about goal setting and success. I talk about what you have to do in order to improve yourself from poor to average, from average to good, from good to great. To have those good years, you have to be able to effect change in the people around you. You are an average coach if you can't effect change. You are a baby-sitter. You are monitoring those players for two or three hours. There are lots of ways to go about effecting change. Some of these things are positive, and some are negative.

Individual drills are important to linebackers. I want to talk to you about my beliefs. Some of the exhibitors in the back aren't going to like this. It is my philosophy on coaching aids. Jack Pardee taught me this. I came from high school to the college level coaching linebackers. Jack was a Hall of Fame pro linebacker, and he was looking over my shoulder at everything I did. My philosophy is this, and he taught it to me: I am not really big on a lot of coaching aids during the season. You have to have certain dummies. You have to have a few cones and sleds. I understand that, but that sled is not going to knock his jock off on Friday night. Jack told me to get all that stuff done during the off-season. He told me I could have one drill with the coaching aid. "Anything past that, and you are out of here." He said he wanted to see them tackling, shedding, striking, covering, and running. He wanted to see them do those things the way they were going to do it on Saturday afternoon. I still use a few things, but not many, and only one a day.

We have a 20-minute, live, get-after-your-butt, special-teams period. That pretty much has our players warmed up before we start the individual periods. Still, there are a few guys each day who are not involved in the special-teams period who need to be warmed up. I'll start the individual period out with some sort of a warm-up. I'm going to emphasize stance and the first step as much as I can at the starting point of that warm-up period. I coach eyes, stance, and first step as they gradually warm up. From there, I am going to some kind of full-speed, ballistic footwork drill. I want a change-of-direction and quick-movement drill to get all the muscles loosened up before we get into the contact period.

Every day, we are going to do certain things. It may be in a different order, but we do it every day. We do an upper-body strike-and-shed drill. We do a lower-body strike-and-shed drill. They learn how to get in a fit position and how to strike with their upper body and shed. They learn how to play the cut block. They strike and shed that block. They are going to learn how to play football through a few coaching aids and a few other bodies.

If you want to know whether your team was ready to play in a game in which you just got your butt kicked, look at the tackling. The number one indicator of whether your team was prepared and ready to play that night is tackling. If they tackled like crap, they weren't prepared. If you are a defensive football coach, you know that doesn't come naturally. Tackling is not natural. It is something you have to work on every single day. I am at the NFL level, and we tackle every day. I'm 38 years old. I've got guys as old as I am, but we are going to tackle every day. You have to emphasize the same points in tackling over and over.

As a defensive football coach, our number one thing is "don't let them score, and get the ball back for the offense." That is it. It is not a hard game. Turnovers don't happen by accident. You have to teach guys how to strip the ball and knock it out. You have to teach them how to intercept the ball. Players in our three major position areas are not allowed to come out of the individual period unless the head coach sees a turnover drill every single day.

I'm very proud that our linebackers are recognized by the league as being the best cover linebackers. I think the reason for that is that I coached in the secondary for a number of years. I couldn't understand why the linebacker coach couldn't get his linebackers to do the same things that our strong safety was doing. The outside linebacker is the same cover man as the strong safety. The linebackers and secondary should be doing the same drill.

A speed turn is used to save time in coverage. When the defensive back is running on the hip of a receiver, he is inside and playing on the upfield hip. The receiver will club, throw the defensive back up the field, and come underneath him. If the defensive back takes the step where he got clubbed, takes another step, then opens up and drives on the receiver, that is three steps. What we teach is to take one step, make a quick head turn, and then come right back on the receiver. We teach our linebacker to do that, and we practice it.

When I came back to the linebackers after coaching the defensive back, I started teaching these big-bodied guys those techniques. They thought I was crazy. They looked like cows falling out of the back of a pickup truck. They were horrible-looking. Now they rival the defensive backs in their technique.

We do a catching drill of some type. How many times does the linebacker get his hands on the football and not finish the catch? Most of the time, the guys in the secondary are receivers who got kicked off the offense. They couldn't catch the damn thing in the first place. The linebackers need the work even more than the defensive backs. Most of those linebackers wished they were tight ends catching touchdown passes. They got moved to defense because they couldn't catch a cold running buck naked in a rainstorm. Because of that, we have to work on their hands every day.

We will pass-rush every day. Those are the drills we do every day. Our individual period every day starts out being 20 minutes. You are bullcrapping yourself if you think we ever get 20 minutes. The first drill that the head coach cuts so that you have time to add whatever he is putting in is the individual period and special-team period. To get all your individual period in, you have to do your drills in combination. Don't do single, one-specific-coaching-area drills. Do two or three specific areas in one drill. Jeff Fisher tells me I have 20 minutes in individual period today, but eight minutes later when he blows the horn to go to the next period, I've got my individual drills all done. I'm still going to do those things that I told you we do every day in eight minutes.

When we get finished, there is a lot of hard breathing going on. We go 100 miles an hour. Let's say we are going over bags today to work on agility. We work on our step-overs and -ups and changes of direction. We work on their eyes while they are going over the dummies. Get in a position where you can see their eyes. If you stand behind them and watch their butts, you are stupid. You have to coach through their eyes to know what they are seeing.

They go down the bags, stepping over them. Then they go up and down them, changing directions. They get on the backside of the bags, and they work on protecting the near arm. They play same arm and same leg protecting against the cut. When they get to the end of the bags, there is a guy there who jumps at them like a frog and tries to cut them. The linebacker plays his hand on the head and turns it. Where the head goes, the body follows. After that, there is a cross-the-bow tackle. I work on agility and cut-block mechanics, get a live rep on the cut block, and make a cross-the-bow tackle. But he still doesn't get an "attaboy" unless he strips the ball on the tackle.

On the tape, you will see us working on the low part of a seven-man sled. We work on upper-body strike. If I work on upper-body strike, I have to concentrate on the hand positioning also. The man who works his hands inside will win the battle. The thumbs have to be up. We have the big muscle groups of the upper body involved. If the thumbs get inside and the wrist rolls back, the wrists get jammed. The plexus of nerves across the tops of the arms shuts off, and you have no upper-body strength. We extend on the dummy with our hands and violently shed it as we go to the next dummy. At the end of the sled, I'll give the guy coming down the sled a live cut block. He has to play the cut live by turning the head, playing the back pad, and flatting him out. The last thing he does is the tackle. We work on strike, explosion, hand placement, and getting his hip across.

You have to be creative. Do combination drills. Don't tell me you don't have enough time. You don't have enough time if you are stupid. There is no place for stupidity in the game. You have to think to stay ahead of the head coach who is going to cut your period short. He is going to fire you if you can't coach. He'll call you in at the end of the year and tell you, "We are going in a different direction." I must get the things taught, regardless of whether he gives me enough time or not.

Here is some philosophical BS for you young coaches. These are the principles of good defense. I believe this and have done it from the junior high level up. First, you have to have great communication in your defense. I'm going to show you something here in a minute on game planning that will make you shake your head. You won't believe we do it. Communication is vital to a defensive football team. You have to communicate, and everyone has to be on the same page.

Second, we coach techniques and give them different types. However, the players have to make the decision on what specific technique to use on a particular down. As an example, I have a 225-pound linebacker. He tries to play "hat and hands" and gets his hands inside on a 340-pound, 7' 9" offensive guard. He gets engulfed and taken down. The officials only call holding when it gets really bad. I'm not going to teach him to play a "hat and hands" technique in this situation. I'm going to teach him a flipper technique. He delivers the flipper and knocks the crap out of that guard. He gets under his pads and gets his body in the hole. He may get buried, but at least the ball is cutting back.

Third, can you effect change? If you want to know the difference between being a good coach and a great coach, this is it. You can't affect their size or speed, but you can effect change. If you can't, you don't need to be coaching. You decide who plays. If he doesn't play at the effort level you want, why in the hell is he playing? That is one thing I want said about me. When people see my linebackers play, they say, "Those guys play all out." If they don't, you will see the next guy going in. I'll get a fresh one in there who is going to bust his butt to get to the ball. The guy I took out comes over yelling at me about his incentive clause for his number of plays. I tell him that if he wants to play and make that incentive clause, he better bust his butt to the ball. If you take a lazy step, you are over by me. He is not going to play unless he plays all out.

In 1993, we were the number one special team in the league. We were very simple as far as scheme. I had seven rookies on that team. We were number one because of effort. They flew to the ball with reckless abandon. You can make that happen. It is a sin if you allow them to take lazy steps.

Finally, intelligence is what we would all like. We would like to have smart players, but I've coached some dumb ones, just as you have. If the dumb guy can play, you've got to find a place for him. Chuck Knox told me this: "If that kid is good enough to play, then you better be smart enough to coach him." It has nothing to do with the kid's intelligence; it has to do with yours. For the ones who aren't very smart, you have to find a way for them to succeed. If they know their own element of what will make the defense successful, they have to do it.

We are a pressure-package defense. We are the only defense in the United States at any level that has the last say. Most offensive teams say they have the last say because they have the automatic system. I'll tell you really quickly how that comes about. Blitzing pressure teams are selling tickets right now. If you have an offensive-minded head coach, he wants you to get the ball back to him in a hurry. I don't want a 14-play drive going on while the All-American quarterback stands on the sideline with his thumb up his butt. The instructions are clear from the head coach: Get the ball back.

If you are a good blitzing team, you have to do the following things:

- You have to disguise.

You don't want the quarterback to know what you are in before the ball is snapped. Make sure your pre-snap is not what you are going to be in after the ball is snapped.

- Timing is important to the blitzing team.

You want to be able to hit the line of scrimmage on the run. If the quarterback sees you creeping, he will chicken out and get rid of the ball. Get the snap count to help with timing. Teams that use motion usually snap the ball at certain points in the motion. Get that from the scouting films. You can use that as a tip-off. Start your blitz when the motion is getting to the area where the ball is snapped.

- You have to collapse the pocket with inside heat.

Buddy Ryan would fire you if he saw an inside pass rusher use a swim move. He wanted the gap ripped and the pocket collapsed.

- Speed pressure comes from the outside.

If the quarterback can step up in the pocket, that is the place where he can escape. If there is no collapse of the pocket, the blitz breaks down. If the speed blitz comes from the inside gap, the ends better be containing.

- You have to take away the quick inside passing game.

Force the offense to run outs and fades. Don't let them throw inside posts and curls.

We are a 4-3 football team, and we like to get into the eight-man force game. We are predominantly an over-and-under shifted team. If we are playing a shade technique on the center and a 3 technique away from the tight end, that is an under front. If we play a 3 technique to the tight end and a shade on the backside, that is an over front. The only way teams get us into a true 4-3 look is if they balance up.

Offensive coordinators who see a team that kicks the front one way or the other will balance up to see if the defense will balance up. This game is not hard. Coaches make it hard. I guess we want to promote our intelligence. If the defense doesn't balance, the quarterback simply counts right and left and runs to the side with the least number of people on it. They use the "check with me" call. What we do is balance up and force you to run to a personnel mismatch rather than a numbers mismatch.

Ninety-nine percent of the time when we break the huddle at the Houston Oilers, I don't know what we are going to play. If I go back and coach at the high school level, I will run this package and system. I'll have to simplify it somewhat, but they can do exactly what we do. We have one of four calls in the huddle. Our game plan is the most important thing we do. We have a two-back formation page. It has every two-back formation known to man on it. We have terminology that describes our communication. The number 212 to us means two wide receivers, one tight end, and two backs. The first number is how many wide receivers, the second is how many tight ends, and the third is how many backs. *Red* means split backs. *Flop* is what Buddy Ryan called the slot set, and that stuck with us. *Brown* is a weak back tilt in the backfield. *Brown-up* is moving the weak back up into a tight slot position off the weak tackle. *I-over* is taking the fullback out of the I and offsetting him strong. *I-under* is moving the fullback the other way. If we moved the fullback up into the slot position, it was *I-under flop* or *I-over flop*. *Blue* is a strong back tilt, and *blue-flop* is moving him into the slot position. These are all the adjustments you can make with two backs in the backfield.

Across the top of our game-plan sheet, we have "AFC." That stands for *automatic front and coverage*. We have a computer system. I brought one of the charts we use. The one I brought is for the red set, or split-back look. On this sheet, we have every run from this formation and the hole they run into. The passes are recorded at the top of the sheet. A split-back formation in our league is primarily a passing set, but they may run a little lead draw strong and weak.

This set is mainly a pass and not a lot of run. We play a seven-man front to it. We are going to take away your wide receivers and force you to beat us with your tight end or your backs. If you run to the openside, we are going to kick the front weak. If you like to run to the tight side, we kick the front strong. We have decided whether you run the opposite of the scouting report; we have won that down. The offense is doing something they really don't want to do. If an offense is multiple, it has tendencies. We do a five- to seven-game breakdown on people we play. In the secondary, we are going to roll the coverage to your best receiver or where you like to throw the ball.

If the offense comes out in a running set, we get into the eight-man front and stop the run. The quickest way to get beat is not being able to stop the run. We have been number one, two, or three in rushing defense in the NFL since I've been at the Houston Oilers. If you are a tight-end-running team, we kick over. If you run to the split end, we kick under. We have one more than you can block either way, and we will kick your butt.

Our BF stands for *blitz the formation*. I call a coach who just picks a blitz a *Rolodex coach*. If you happen to call the wrong blitz, you have a corner somewhere on that field trying to cover their best receiver all over the field. You have lost. We want to blitz and guarantee a hit on the quarterback.

We study your protection. If we know that you are going to get three out to the strongside, we use that to our advantage. The third receiver strong is a hot receiver. We know that the center is blocking weak and that the split back is check-releasing weak. We know that the quarterback is reading the fourth rusher strong as his hot read. Our blitz is coming from the fourth strong attitude. The lesser corner can take away the inside. He knows that all he has to play is a six-yard stem. The ball is coming off; otherwise the quarterback is on his back. The defense has a free rusher.

We know whether you have the potential to block eight. When you do that, we bring nine. We have to have a free blitz man coming so that the corner is guaranteed heat and only has to cover the short route. We get there in a hurry, or we get beat in a hurry. We don't have to die that slow death with the quarterback standing back there baking a pizza.

When I was in high school, we double-called our coverage. We played one or the other, depending on the set. Ten of the players got the check, and one didn't. All he listened to was what was called in the huddle. He played the first call and not the second. What we do is this: All 11 break the huddle, and none of them know what is going on. Here is the huddle call: "AFDC, ready, break." They have to listen to the communications that are going on as the offense comes out to set up. They have to hear the Mike linebacker and free safety, and they all have to be on the same page. Otherwise, we are going to have a really crappy down. The thought process isn't that far out of whack. We put up the best front that we can when you are going to run the ball and the best coverage when you throw it.

Tuesday is the off day for our players. That is in the collective bargaining agreement. That is when we put together the game plan. That is when we put together the formations, tendencies, runs, and passes. On Wednesday, we work on first- and second-down calls. On Thursday, we repeat the hard first- and second-down calls and work really hard on the third-down calls. On Friday, we throw all the crap at them, which includes goal line, short yardage, and that kind of stuff. On Saturday, we review, and we play on Sunday.

In the drill part of linebacker play, we use these types of drills. We talk about defeating a block. We talk about defending area responsibility against a run. We drill them in gap control. We give them a pass coverage key, zone or man-to-man. The last thing we talk about is pursuit.

Two things before I start the film. I always felt that if I could take one thing home from each guy who spoke, I had had a hell of a clinic. I learned a lot of things, even if it was just a different way to say the things I was doing. If it makes the kid understand because the new way is more descriptive, that is worth it. Here is the first thing Jack Pardee taught me. A linebacker is an in-between player. He has to be tough enough to play the run and have enough finesse to play the pass. The in-between player has to be coached this way. He lines up to stop the run and reacts to the pass, or he plays pass coverage keys and reacts to the run, but he is not going to do both. You are doing that linebacker an injustice if you are not coaching him that way.

Your defensive call on first down is a run call. We are in an eight-man front, playing run as a linebacker and reacting to our pass coverage. That gives the linebacker a jump on making a big play. I want a playmaker, not a robot. If I have to coach that linebacker very much, he is probably not a linebacker. The game is easy. Find the guy with the ball, and go splatter that sucker. Go intercept the ball when it is thrown. If he has instincts, don't screw them up. Don't give him so many things to think about that he can't play. Give him a run key, and let him run to the ball. If the offense gives him a "high hat" (that is pass blocking to us), he reacts and goes to pass coverage. The same thing is true of the pass key. The linebacker gets his pass key and gets into his coverage. If for some reason he were to get a run key, he reacts to the run.

The second thing is pad level. How many of us have said this over and over? "The guy with the lowest pads is going to win." You win with pad level. You have to get your pads underneath his pads. As the player gets down in his stance, he is thinking about whether his pad level is under his opponent's. The next thing he knows, he is on his back. Kids don't make a mistake on purpose. They make a mistake because they don't know what to do. They are trying to do what you tell them to do, but they don't know how. So you turn the film on. If you are not using a film every day in practice, you are stupid. The reason you watch the film is to see the body position. His line of sight is down, and he thinks his pads might be under the opponent's. Give him a horizontal look. Now, you ask him, "Are your eyes at his throat?" If the linebacker's eyes are not at the blocker's throat, he is too high. He can look straight ahead.

I talked about exploding their eyes on contact. Watch their eyes as they tackle. Do they explode the eyes through the contact, or do they cringe on contact and blink? Get to a point where you can see their eyes. If the linebacker can always see the throat, he is going to win at pad level.

We play a lot of eight-man front and get a lot of zone scoop blocking. We never allow both parts of the scoop. We are going to hold the man on the line of scrimmage and allow the linebacker to run downhill into the gap. If the blocker gives an avoid step and tries to play wide on the scoop to get to the linebacker, we use the momentum for the blocker to pull us away from the backside scoop block. We grab the hip of the first blocker and pull through to beat the back scoop block. They may get the down lineman blocked or the linebacker blocked, but they are never going to get both halves of the scoop blocked.

If people do a good job of getting the front seven blocked, the last guy they are going to block is the trail defender on the backside. If they leave him unblocked, we'll chase you down from there. We plug the hell out of the plays on the frontside and make you cut back. When you do, that backside defender will knock the hell out of you and might cause a fumble. In our league, they use these pencil-necked wide receivers to block the backside. We never hold force on a wide receiver. When they come across in motion, they bring a corner with them in our scheme. The corner replaces the linebacker in force, so he can wrong-arm the wide receiver, get inside, and come laterally down the line of scrimmage.

Let's talk really quickly about pass rush. Study the great speed rushers. Who do you think told me all this stuff? Nobody told me this. I study films. You better get the film of the best team in your league and find out why they are kicking your butt. They probably know something you don't know. I get films of guys who are great speed rushers off the edge and watch them. He can fight centrifugal force. He is able to dip and rip and shorten the distance to the pocket. They have the ability to fight the pressure inside. They have the ability at the hip joint to plant and get the toe pointed to where they are going. If the toe is pointed outside and I get blocked outside, that is where I am going. It doesn't matter whether I am bigger and stronger. To fight the pressure, I have to get my cleats in the ground, get under his pads, and be able to run the line I want to. He has to fight with pressure to get his toe pointed and his hips turned in. With each step of my front foot, I have to get more cleats in the ground. We buy three eight-foot sections of PVC pipe and connect them in circles. We practice rushing around them. We make them chase one another in the warm-up drills. We use these circles and incorporate them into our sack-and-strip drill.

We have dummies with Velcro arms on them. We normally put a ball in them. As the linebackers are speed-rushing, they take the inside, upfield shoulder and wrap up the tackle. The downfield arm is stripping the ball. If they get the ball stripped out, they are scooping and scoring with the ball. If the numbers of our players to theirs are even, we want to scoop and score. If the numbers are in their favor, get on the ball and recover it. We are working on a half-moon speed rush: knocking the ball out, scooping, and scoring. We try to pick the ball up and get it in the center of our body. We don't want them to try to pick the ball up outside the frame of the body. They straddle the ball when they pick it up. Then we have a race to the end zone. Make sure you spike it at the end. That is simple stuff, but they have to work on it too.

To teach the linebacker how to play over a tight end, I put him in a fit position. I put him in a position where his hands are on the inside and the tight end's hands are outside. I start with their arms collapsed. That is to simulate the tight end firing off and engulfing the linebacker. The linebacker's eyes are at the tight end's throat. His hands are inside, and his thumbs are up. He wants his feet in a good power base. From this point right here, I have to teach them to separate and shed. We call the drill *fit, separate, and shed*. From this point, I work on extending his arms, getting his hips back, and getting his head to the outside. If the tight end starts to walk on the linebacker, the linebacker keeps a firm arm in the direction he is going. He takes three steps with the tight end and violently sheds him. From there, he gets in position to tackle.

The next thing we do is to put the tight end's hands down and let him come off. The linebacker has to fight for the inside hand position, get his hips and body away, and power-clean the tight end. Then he repeats the first drill. I have added to the drill because we got a new tight end coach who is working as hard as I am with his tight ends. I had to develop another part to this drill to work on beating the tight end's hands. I put two guys on a line. They are going for a three-second count. One guy starts with his hands inside. When I say "go," the other guy tries to get his hands inside. They